Cover design by Alexander Philip

Cover images courtesy of

John Beardsworth & Levitt Parkes

Foreword

A philosopher once said that those who fail to learn from history are doomed to repeat it, which is why a work such as this is important, as it draws attention to a formative period in our nation's history. The period between 1640 and 1660, known variously as The British Civil Wars, The War of the Three Kingdoms or more commonly The English Civil Wars, was one of significance in the evolution of the country we see today.

Most people will be aware that our modern Parliamentary system effectively began with them but less well known is its impact in other areas. Away from the political arena the precursors of other institutions can be found. Already almhouses were in existence but the scale of the wars led to both sides setting up the first military hospitals to treat sick or injured soldiers. This early foray into health care was built on after the Restoration by Charles II's formation of the Royal Hospital Chelsea, further developing the idea of the state looking after the old and infirm. At the same time the newssheets and pamphlets which proliferated to feed the hunger for information from a surprisingly literate population was the beginning of the newspaper industry we see today, not least in the emergence of partisan publications pushing the propaganda of one party or another.

The modern Sealed Knot was founded when Brigadier Peter Young, feeling the military history of the period had been somewhat neglected, wrote the first serious study of the Battle of Edgehill. This was published in 1968 and as a publicity exercise he held a party where he asked guests to dress up in costume from the period. This was enjoyed so much that they wanted to continue doing so and the result was the founding of our Society which has now been going for more than 50 years. The very first principle in its Memoranda and Articles of Incorporation reads: "To promote research into and the study of and public interest in history …" helping to address the concerns of the philosopher mentioned above.

Whilst the Society focusses heavily on the military aspects of the Civil Wars, not least through the large scale battle re-enactments it puts on, it has also stimulated a significant and increasing volume of work studying the various aspects of the period. Alongside this, as one of the very first re-enactment groups, it helped to kick start what is now a wide spectrum of re-enactment groups of all sizes and periods of history.

Poetry, rhyme and doggerel all played their part in the Civil Wars. At one end there are works by the likes of Andrew Marvell and John Milton and at the other doggerel rhymes used as crude propaganda by all parties. There is even the possibility that some of our modern nursery rhymes refer to events from them, for example Humpty Dumpty. In turn this means that this work by Colin Croad is particularly apt as it draws attention using the medium of rhyme.

Simon Wright

 **Chair, The Sealed Knot, November 2020**
www.thesealedknot.org.uk
www.facebook.com/thesealedknot/
info@thesealedknot.org.uk

The English Civil War

By C.S. Croad

Introduction.

I can clearly remember how excited I was when the 1970 film 'Cromwell' was shown on television for the first time. I had to wait for it to come on the TV as my parents couldn't afford to send all their five sons to the cinema, so when I did finally manage to see it I was overjoyed! I was probably at the end of middle school when I saw it, and our history lessons had already dipped into the civil war, so I considered myself something of an expert. As I watched the star cast doing their best to portray all those important characters from that period, I never thought to question the film's authenticity or accuracy. I was young and too engrossed with the battle scenes to tell myself that perhaps they'd taken artistic interpretation a bit too far. To me, the film was English history at its bloody and dramatic best.

It was only in later years, after reading several good books on the subject, that I began to see the real English Civil War with all its complexities and gruesome consequences. Percentage wise, no war has claimed more English lives than this one. Politically speaking, few events in history have had such a dramatic impact on England's turbulent path to modernity. The consequences for every level of society, for every city, town, village and hamlet was truly life changing. Families were divided by it, friends became enemies overnight and the innocent, as always, were caught squarely in the middle, watching their communities and livelihoods go up in smoke or captured by hostile forces.

The legacy of the civil war is seen by the number of people who enjoy recreating a famous battle, making great efforts to produce replica uniforms and weaponry to make sure they look the part. Some years ago a neighbour of mine was overjoyed when he showed me his latest acquisition, a perfect replica of a Roundhead cavalry helmet, that iconic lobster pot which appears so often in films, documentaries or books. Today there are many respectable organisations which strive to keep the memory, and passion, of that era alive, albeit without the blood, pain and disease. Most of us will have seen news footage of men in a whole variety of uniforms marching and manoeuvring across a field to the accompaniment of shouts of encouragement from admiring crowds or to the narration of the organiser over the loudspeaker system. People still have an interest in watching and supporting the side they want to see win; such is the interest to this day. Even those who know relatively little about the era, if stopped in the street and asked, would probably tell you they see themselves as either Roundhead or Cavalier. Yet, with the benefit of living so many centuries later, with all its political and social development, we can now look back objectively and see that both sides had a good point to make. For the king, the inheritor of centuries of royal privilege and belief in his divine appointment, it was a matter of convincing his parliament that their new and radical ideas were out of place with the natural order of things, that he knew best because God had ordained it so. For the radicals, who wanted change and saw the divine right of Kings as something from the middle ages, they hoped to make their monarch accept that they were no longer living in the dark ages, and that change was inevitable, but not at the expense of the throne. Indeed, the last thought on anyone's mind was the abolition of the monarchy. With such radical, and fundamentally opposite points of view, it was only a matter of time before both sides clashed.

So, who ultimately won this struggle for supremacy? The forces of Parliament obviously won the war, but in many ways they lost the peace through trying to force their ideas of how best to live, and worship God, onto a nation of people who just wanted to heal the wounds and try to enjoy life after such an apocalyptic event. For most, life could be hard enough without also being instructed on how they should live it. In the end, the Royalists won with the restoration of Charles the Second, putting paid to any further ideas of a Republic. However, the nation had changed forever, and the relationship between monarch and Parliament would never be the same again, and though Charles the Second would try to carry on where his father left off, he was wise enough to realise that his Commons could only be pushed so far. What's more, the defiant spirit of Parliament had never truly been eliminated and would show itself again when James the Second came to the throne, resulting in the Glorious Revolution and the ousting of the last Stuart King.

Though no one could see it at the time, ultimately it was the people and the political structure of the nation which came out on top, and set the foundations for our modern constitutional monarchy, born out of anxiety, blood and pain. Like every birth, there is a degree of pain and uncertainty, but from that pain a new democracy was ultimately born, one which has influenced and shaped nations across the world.

This poem tells the story of how King and Parliament talked, negotiated and finally fought each other to prove a point. Both were immovable in their beliefs, both political and religious, but only at the end of the war did those on Parliament's side make up their mind that their king, and the role of King, must go. In our modern age, with the threat of religious fundamentalists doing us harm, it might come as a sobering thought to realise that this same religious fundamentalism was responsible for much of the terror which took place across all of Europe during much of the seventeenth century, and England's counties did not escape it either.

If it appears that I have written too much and too long about any particular character, then I apologise in advance for what might seem to be bias but isn't really. The two main characters which most people know about are King Charles and Oliver Cromwell, so they do appear quite often in the story. Others are also mentioned in detail as they were instrumental in the events which played out. What's more, the reader will notice that one of the main figures, Cromwell, doesn't appear in any detail until much later in the story, as his role early on was minor, whilst Charles is mentioned almost throughout. When I do begin to write about Cromwell in detail it is merely to put his role into context. So, to all those Roundheads and Royalists who read the poem please believe my attempts to maintain that all important objectivity, essential for any history book.

It is a somewhat long and detailed story, but interesting too. It is well worth the reading, as it perhaps gives an insight into the reason why people today still associate themselves with either Roundhead or Cavalier, Parliament or Monarch. At the end of the poem, I have included a short quiz which will help you, the reader, to decide which one you may have chosen to support if you had lived back then. There are no right or wrong answers, and it is just for fun, but it might help you think about the dilemma many people faced.

Index:

After the Tudors

When Elizabeth the first finally died,

She hadn't an heir for the throne supplied,

So the crown would go to the Scottish King,

Who had a legitimate claim to bring.

The house of Stuart was Scottish born,

And would the English court adorn,

With hope that England wouldn't descend,

Into the strife that fear might send.

For James of Scotland seemed to be,

The only true choice that England could see,

To make a smooth, peaceful transition,

To thwart those nobles with much ambition.

So, James the first of England arrived,
And hopes for a dynasty were revived,
When the people saw he had a son,
Who'd rule one day when father was done.

Raised in the faith of the Scottish kirk,
James thought he had to do much work,
In making the people of England accept,
That he as a king was wise and adept.

Coins in his image were rapidly minted,
A beautiful Bible in English printed,
Hoping these acts would clearly show,
How a righteous King could grace bestow.

What's more, the kirk had left on him,
A strict belief, firm and grim,
Making James a religious terror,
Punishing Catholics he saw in error.

Such was the feeling and terrible fear,

That Catholics suffered should they adhere,

To their beliefs and then be caught,

Being hunted, it seemed, just for sport.

The fear of Catholics spread through the land,

And James was determined to take them in hand,

To try to put an end to their threat,

To catch as many as he could in his net.

Yet soon resistance would take shape,

To help the Catholic faith escape,

From all their pain and persecution,

Born from the King's quick execution.

A plot to destroy Parliament's members,

Blowing them and the King to fiery embers,

A band of Catholics who were intent,

On showing James what terror meant.

But the gunpowder plot was soon uncovered,

The King and Parliament's fate recovered.

Just in time the plot was spoiled,

And protestant fear of Catholics boiled.

So James continued to rule as he thought,

Regardless of what his actions brought.

Though King, he felt a constant suspicion,

That no one accepted his royal position.

Yet Charles, his son, would follow on,

When James, his father, was finally gone.

Charles would hope to rule and thrive,

Ascending in sixteen twenty-five.

In sixteen hundred, Charles was born,

But, at three, was rudely torn,

From his family when his father became,

The King of England to much acclaim.

Weak and sickly from his birth,

Few could see the prince's worth,

So Charles was kept back at home,

Until gaining the strength so he could roam.

At barely four, he was duly sent,

To England's court where he'd present,

Himself to England's nobility,

Greeted to smiles and civility.

Yet he couldn't quite shake his hesitant speech,

A stammer which family would beseech,

Young Charles to do his best to conceal,

As they thought it lacked a charm and appeal.

As the second son of the king and queen,

The face of Charles was rarely seen,

As all attention went to his brother,

Henry Frederick who the court would smother.

Charles thought his brother the perfect prince,

And didn't need courtiers to try and convince,

That Henry, as king, would be great,

But wicked and cruel was Henry's fate.

For when eighteen, Henry had died,

With the grief at court for James' pride,

For father, mother and brother too,

Lamented his loss, and their grief was true.

All of a sudden, their sickly child,

At twelve, would have to be schooled and styled,

As heir apparent with a new title,

His role in the dynasty now being vital.

Portrait of a King

When young, Prince Charles never supposed,

That the role of king would be proposed,

For he was the second son of James,

Never to hold those royal names.

In sixteen twenty-five, Charles was crowned,

And to the rule of England bound,

With people not knowing what this would entail,

Hoping that order and peace might prevail.

His father championed the protestant cause,

Dealing with Catholics without pause,

So, people hoped that Charles the first,

Would keep those feelings his father had nursed.

Long before his calling dawned,

His role as prince by James was pawned,

Hoping to gain alliance with Spain,

An act the people held in disdain.

King James thought Charles could be a match,

To the Spanish Infanta, and would be a catch,

But negotiations would fall apart,

As the Princess disliked him from the start.

The puritan part of England's belief,

Were filled with suspicion, fear and grief,

That James sought alliance through a Catholic bride,

A Protestant king who'd damaged their pride.

But in the end, he would marry,

A Bourbon princess who would carry,

Her Catholic faith to the throne,

Feeding suspicions and setting the tone.

Henrietta Maria of Catholic France,

Whom Charles would marry through fickle chance,

Would be seen as a thorn in his side,

In a Protestant England where she couldn't hide.

Having met Henrietta while he passed,

Through Paris when the spell was cast,

Charles felt sure there was a detection,

Of interest and some small affection.

When the deal with Spain had fallen through,

The course of Charles towards France blew.

Convinced of Henrietta's charm,

They wed by proxy at Notre Dame.

But protestant England would never trust,

Their king and Queen as people must,

And every time the king did wrong,

Thoughts of Catholic plots were long.

Like monarchs before, Charles believed,

The role of the King by God was conceived,

Thinking that what he did was right,

Regardless of anyone else's plight.

Yet England was home to those who were,

Filled with the zeal of the righteous and pure,

Of men and women who knew their god,

Would punish their king for not sparing the rod.

This was a time of religious zeal,

When the presence of God was near and real.

Protestant puritans who dearly craved,

To see God's face and then to be saved.

So, having a Catholic for their Queen,

Many believed it was a screen,

For catholic influence in the reign,

Which Charles had added to their pain.

With dreams of a protestant queen then crushed,

And then a marriage to a catholic rushed,

Some saw the new queen as an outsider,

A catholic and a protestant derider.

Yet the king was sure that God had set,

His plans in place that His will be met,

To make the nation a better place,

Which the people of England should accept and embrace.

Believing he only did God's will,

Charles would rule with little skill,

Making people begin to think,

That the monarch was leading them to the brink.

But despite professing God's affection,

His actions only caused objection,

As the court of Charles was seen as depraved,

Filled with those who to lusts were enslaved.

A king indulged his courtiers desire,

To live in luxury and never tire,

Of masques which often went too far,

Debauched, outrageous and so bizarre.

All were encouraged to exceed and excel,

Caught up in the party's magic spell,

With costumes designed to impress and to shock,

Hoping their peers would stare and take stock.

Charles had developed slowly when young,

Not swift of wit or nimble of tongue,

And despite the efforts to help with his grammar,

He always retained his hesitant stammer.

Those around him didn't care,

So long as Charles had favours to spare.

With words of advice to speak in his ear,

Hoping that Charles would keep them near.

23

The one who was the court's foremost,

Was the Duke of Buckingham, who was engrossed,

In keeping his place once James was dead,

Remaining the favourite and keeping ahead.

Yet, nothing would alter or distract,

The king of England from the fact,

That he believed God was his guide,

Always present and on his side.

Charles and Parliament

Never far from Charles' side,

Buckingham stirred the prince's pride,

Stating war with Spain must surely follow,

If marriage rejection they'd have to swallow.

But when the war was duly declared,

English pride wasn't spared,

As lack of funds and bad leadership,

Saw Buckingham fail in generalship.

It was bad enough that the duke had stirred,

Charles to the brink where war was spurred,

But when the young prince gained a French bride,

His concessions to France were not long to hide.

For Charles had promised much to the French,

Hoping the catholic fears to quench,.

Making a hoped-for secret deal,

To help English Catholics under the heel.

The House of Commons soon reacted,

In a statement of protest which was protracted.

But Charles refused to dismiss his friend,

Who he'd praise, and always commend.

So, instead of sacking the hated duke,

Charles gave Parliament a bad rebuke,

Allowing his friend in the court to stay,

Dismissing Parliament, sending it away.

But in March of sixteen twenty-eight,

Parliament was summoned to debate,

The right of the king to levy a tax,

Which Parliament thought a dangerous act.

Then Parliament's long Petition of Rights,

Set the House of Commons' sights,

On how the king should be contained,

And rights of Parliament were maintained.

This petition clearly displayed,

That Parliament would try to blockade,

Their king should he try to participate,

In acts he might try or anticipate.

And Charles and his queen soon fell out,

When he, due to faith, began to doubt,

That her Catholic practise caused no harm,

Giving him and his subjects some alarm.

Charles then broke the deal he agreed,

Sent troops to La Rochelle to make France Bleed,

In defence of the Huguenots who, Charles said,

Were Protestants fighting the catholic dread.

But Buckingham was in charge once more,

When the English approached the foreign shore,

And yet again the plan went astray,

The duke, once more, losing the day.

Charles needed cash to fund the campaign,

Putting the nation under strain,

By declaring to all there would be a forced loan,

Causing the people to lament and to moan.

A tax without his Parliament's approving,

Caused Parliament's anger and its reproving.

Through due process, they tried to appeal,

Though Charles, to Parliament, wouldn't kneel.

But Parliament didn't have long to wait,

When in August Buckingham met his fate,

When an assassin made his move,

The hatred of the realm to prove.

Charles was distraught, and could not bear,

To lose the man who shared his care.

For two whole days he stayed in his room,

Alone and lamenting in sumptuous gloom.

But the people of England loudly rejoiced,

Their joy at the death of the duke loudly voiced.

The duke, an adviser and emotional crutch,

Showed the people that Charles was well out of touch.

But the marriage to Henrietta improved,

Once the Duke of Buckingham was removed.

Soon, the queen was expecting a child,

And their relationship was no longer wild.

The child she carried would be the heir,

If God and disease would hopefully spare.

A boy, they hoped, would follow on,

Who would the crown of England don.

Parliament Isn't Needed

In January sixteen twenty-nine,

Parliament, by Charles' grand design,

Was opened when he gave a speech,

Hoping the MP's minds to reach.

Tonnage and poundage was a tax introduced,

Centuries before that wealth be produced,

From goods that were daily imported,

But the tax, over years, had become distorted.

King James had also supplemented,

Extra tax which trade tormented.

And the custom that the king imposed,

By Charles' Parliament was opposed.

They declared the extra custom illegal,

Although King Charles had a right most regal,

Stating the issue must be redressed,

Before the issue could be addressed.

Some felt the imposition of these dues,

Was against the Petition of Rights and views,

Which said that Parliament should hold power,

Not be the king's puppet and simply cower.

Charles then called for the House to adjourn,

But MP's knew the king wouldn't learn,

Unless they acted and showed what they felt,

So they had to move fast that the lesson be dealt.

The Speaker of the House was held in his chair,

To give MP's the time to dare,

To pass three acts against their lord,

Furthering the growth of the rising discord.

The acts were read out, and well received,

As those in the House mostly believed,

That Charles would have to do as they bid,

Not thinking that Charles would do as he did.

For the king was angry, and retaliated,

In a way which simply illustrated,

His belief in his right to do as he felt,

Regardless of consequence, or what actions spelt.

Charles simply had his Parliament dissolved,

Believing his problems would be resolved.

To also show that he must be obeyed,

Nine members of Parliament were arrested and paid.

Locked up and imprisoned, each was a martyr,

Punished for believing in Parliament's charter,

That they, not the king, should make legislation,

That many, not one, is best for the nation.

Without a Parliament to raise more tax,

Charles' was forced his wars to relax,

Seeking with Spain and France a bad peace,

Lest his nation's defeats quickly increase.

Though a king had ruled by himself before,

The centuries had brought about new law,

Giving Parliament the right to raise the finances,

Which the king soon discovered in new circumstances.

Now Charles' funds would have to be found,

From customary income from estates all around,

Drawing the wealth from the lands he controlled,

Scratching around for the wealth and the gold.

There was one method which Charles could use,

An ancient right which he'd soon abuse,

A tax by which he could stave off debt,

But which by protests would be met.

Ship money was seen as a lucrative way,

Where Charles could raise the funds to pay,

For his court and the lifestyle he deserved,

As the tax was a right for monarchs reserved.

A medieval tax in times of war,

On towns around the English shore,

Now the king would spread the net,

Seeing the wealth which he could get.

His tax collectors found their prey,

Making every Town to pay,

Ship money tax to help finance,

Any expense or dalliance.

At once the people were outraged,

That this plan by Charles should be staged.

Yet only a few were so outspoken,

As the king thought Parliament finished, broken.

He also found an extra income,

By granting monopolies to raise the sum,

Which hoped to make his finances better,

So he wouldn't be anyone's debtor.

Through this, patent holders were duly charged,

To have sole rights on goods enlarged,

Giving them the right to charge any price,

A plan which would the rich entice.

In Scotland he'd earned great damnation,

By the earlier Act of Revocation,

Where gifts of royal land were revoked,

Leaving the Scottish people provoked.

And borders of royal forests were restored,

Charles acting as a new landlord,

Fining the people who were on his new land,

Or selling the forests so his wealth could expand.

Despite all these moves which some felt abrupt,

Charles was struggling and was almost bankrupt.

The City of London refused a loan,

Causing the king and his courtiers to moan.

So the Tower of London's bullion was seized,

As desperate Charles each avenue squeezed.

The East India Company stock was taken,

To pay the king's debts, leaving them shaken.

For eleven long years, Charles ruled by himself,

His Parliament dormant, stuck on the shelf.

With absolute power, he ruled supreme,

Believing it was God's perfect dream.

A Heavy Hand

England was full of prominent men,

Intellectual, zealous and swift with the pen,

Who believed their path to God was revealed,

When the break with Catholic Rome was sealed.

The Protestant faith was slowly supplied,

With pious men who identified,

Heresies to their faith which was driven,

By God who had enlightenment given.

Religious men and women sought,

A purer faith that couldn't be bought,

By traditional trappings of pomp and show,

Preferring instead a simpler flow.

The Puritans were a zealous sect,

Who grew in number and hoped to correct,

All those practises they saw as wrong,

Preaching the gospel through sermon and song.

The thirty-nine articles of the Tudor era,

Had sought to make their faith much clearer,

By giving King Henry's break with Rome,

Common worship and a settled home.

England and church wouldn't be the same,

As slowly English religion became,

Different but of the same belief,

The articles meant for England's relief.

Yet over the century since it was defined,

Puritan thoughts had been refined,

And people in England had chosen a form,

That to some of the bishops wasn't the norm.

So in November, sixteen twenty-eight,

Charles evoked the Puritan hate,

When the thirty-nine articles were re-submitted,

With the bishop's power to chastise permitted.

In it, the King had duly declared,

That all deviation would not be spared,

And the state religion would chastise,

All deviation they saw in their eyes.

The Protestant Book of Common Prayer,

Would have to be followed or else beware,

As Charles and his bishops were ready to pounce,

With acts of punishment to pronounce.

Woe betide those who spoke out of turn,

As branding or fining would make them learn,

That the king was ready to set an example,

And on dissenters to brutally trample.

Puritan believers were clearly marked,

The fire of outrage within them sparked,

As this was a move which convinced them all,

That Catholic influence would see them fall.

Then Charles turned attention to the place of his birth,

Believing that Scotland was ready and worth,

The effort of making the Scottish Kirk change,

Believing he could their faith rearrange.

In sixteen hundred and thirty-three,

Charles saw the Scots bend their knee,

Becoming their king, lord and master,

Yet, now their king was courting disaster.

So Charles sent word and duly insisted,

That Scotland's faith in which they persisted,

Should now to the English church conform,

Hoping that Scotland's Kirk would transform.

But the Scots were not in the mood to give in,

Believing that change would be a great sin,

And they questioned why the king might think,

He could change their traditions with paper and ink.

Fiercely defensive for what they held true,

The Scots weren't long in expressing their view,

Speaking out at what they perceived,

Was just interference, leaving many aggrieved.

Long before, the Scots had agreed,

That their kirk was in dire need,

To see reform and so they responded,

With people and God together bonded.

Each made a covenant before their maker,

To be bound to God and not a foresaker,

Of the new faith which they seized,

And which through all the members breathed.

This covenant with God was reaffirmed,

As national outrage was confirmed,

With the English practice soundly rejected,

Its English ways deeply suspected.

The Scottish kirk was sacred, revered,

Protestant followers in doctrine reared,

Evolving to something of which they were proud,

So interference would not be allowed.

Charles saw his rights put to the test,

By Scottish outrage and words of unrest,

So he raised an army and sent it north,

Without even summoning his Parliament forth.

Charles hoped to catch the Scots unawares,

As Scots debated religious cares,

But at Berwick the English army halted,

Without a shot fired, no lines assaulted.

For Charles now feared that his army was weak,

So decided instead to negotiate, speak,

Hoping to reach some good compromise,

Or at least not to lose face in their eyes.

But Charles was cunning, and hoped to raise cash,

To send bigger forces to win and smash,

All resistance that his troops might engage,

And his rights as king to enforce and assuage.

From Catholic Spain he arranged to borrow,

Much needed wealth, but the deal was hollow,

For the Spanish ships were apprehended,

By the Dutch Navy, and plans were suspended.

So the talks of peace remained on the table,

As Charles realised that he wasn't able,

To raise the money to enforce his will,

Reluctantly swallowing a bitter pill.

For the king now saw what he had to do,

If he, to his heart, were to be true,

Recalling the House, which was the centre,

Of Charles' restrictions and willing tormentor.

Short & Long Parliament

Royalist sympathies were still quite strong,

Believing that power should still belong,

To the king whatever problems arose,

Following along each path he chose.

.

Yet the king had clearly demonstrated,

His ruling should be moderated,

By others who might have the vision,

To see each problem and division.

Despite his heavy hand approach,

The fear of debt would still encroach,

Leaving his plans badly tattered,

Hopes of successful leadership scattered.

Facing debt, Charles had no choice,

But to seek his Parliament's voice,

In giving assent on granting him cash,

Exposed to their words and a firm backlash.

Although the king could always count,

On the House of Lords who'd always mount,

A keen defence for his royal person,

Hoping his status wouldn't worsen.

Yet there were those in the House of Lords,

Who saw the problem and leaned towards,

The House of Commons and what they stood for,

And the fears of the people which they bore.

Whatever laws and Acts were passed,

Whatever accusations were cast,

The Lords would have to soon decide,

To challenge their king, or his ways abide.

In March sixteen forty, Parliament convened,

With true intentions carefully screened,

Longing to work to their objective,

Not just to Charles' own directive.

For Parliament had only been recalled,

When Charles' war with the Scots was stalled,

Only wanting to use all the MP's

Believing they'd grant his desire with ease.

Yet Parliament hadn't forgotten a thing,

Clearly aggrieved and remembering,

All the trouble they'd had in the past,

Thinking they had the king at last.

The house agreed to grant revenue,

Giving respect to the king that was due,

If the 'ship money' tax was amended,

If the hated tax was finally ended.

Charles was having to face their nerve,

Demands from which they wouldn't swerve.

Clearly, they hadn't their grievance forgotten,

Their firm defiance having stronger gotten.

In March, there was a general election,

Which caused the king much sad reflection,

As candidates of Charles lost their seats,

Causing much gossip on London's streets.

For Parliament wanted more concessions,

Were daring with their loud expressions,

Trying to make the king concede,

To see, at last, the nation's need.

Two of Charles' friends pursued,

To broker a deal they thought was shrewd.

The Earls of Northumberland and Strafford failed,

To get the king money when plans were unveiled.

They said the king might soon relent,

On 'ship money' tax if cash was sent,

To his court for his Scottish attack,

To keep the king's offensive on track.

Yet Parliament could not give it's backing,

As a general consensus was found to be lacking.

The House was filled with a loud commotion,

With the wrath of Charles being set in motion.

Having the House of Lords support,

Charles felt his case could still be fought,

So Parliament, again, was duly dismissed,

Causing outrage in his Parliament's midst.

For less than a month, the MP's had sat,

Their hopes for reform soon falling flat,

As Charles, yet again, showed them all,

Parliament was there for his beck and call.

The Earl of Strafford, by now, was seen,

The king's confidant next to the queen.

With Parliament gone, he set in place,

Thorough plans to empower his grace.

Being the king's right-hand man,

Strafford envisaged a daring plan,

To make the king's power more efficient,

A central authority less deficient.

He and the king took their army north,

When Scotland's Parliament had come forth,

With a statement saying they'd rule alone,

When seeds of suspicion had rapidly grown.

But Strafford and Charles were ill prepared,

Their army unfit, and the Scots were not scared.

The Scottish Covenanter army moved south,

The fear being spread by word of mouth.

Both forces met near a place called Newburn,

Where the English army would have to learn,

What it meant to face a veteran force,

Who defeated the English without remorse.

Demands at home for the Parliament grew,

So Charles and Strafford had the view,

That they would have to act with speed,

With skill and statesmanship proceed.

But Charles convened the Lords instead,

A council of peers with him as head,

But, by the time it met in September that year,

Charles began to consensus adhere.

The king announced that he would allow,

Parliament to meet, and powers endow,

To resolve the war in England's favour,

Determined never to flinch or waiver.

Yet Parliament wouldn't meet until later,

And Scots were still seen as the north's violator,

With an army that stood on English soil,

Free to roam and the lands to despoil.

So Charles asked his peers what he should do,

As fears for the north of England grew.

The peers agreed that peace should be made,

Though many in England felt angry, betrayed.

November, sixteen forty, England would see,

Parliament assemble to debate and agree,

On how they could work to at last prevent,

Disbandment of Parliament with the king's assent.

Elections were held, and the king's supporters,

Lost seats in the House in many quarters.

Much royal propaganda was heard and spun,

With just one hundred and forty-three seats won.

Three hundred and fifty seats were held,

By Parliamentarians, whose numbers swelled.

Most to the king weren't well disposed,

And, almost at once, change was proposed.

With a majority, change could be designed,

The fervour for justice not allowed to be blind.

They'd waited too long to have their say,

Showed their resolve without delay.

The king's right-hand man by the House was reached,

When he, for treason, was quickly impeached.

In Strafford there was a man they saw,

Who helped King Charles think he had no flaw.

So Parliament voted, and he was arrested,

The right hand of Charles, who MP's detested,

Forcing Charles to sign the warrant,

An act the king found really abhorrent.

For Charles was sending a friend to the grave,

A loyal noble he wanted to save,

But Parliament voted, and the king acquiesced,

Signing his name leaving Charles much distressed.

MP's power seemed to know no bounds,

As the House would echo to voice and sounds,

Of a Parliament which with life was filled,

As its breath of life into England spilled.

Soon the Commons would have to debate,

England's condition and Parliament's fate.

But previous sessions only indicated,

How Charles had bullied and dictated.

Now MP's would try to find a solution,

To bolster this ancient institution,

By giving it power not to be shunned,

Leaving the king and his courtiers stunned.

In sixteen forty-one, they gained a new lease,

Whereby it's influence might start to increase,

Giving MP's a much better chance,

To have more say, and it's say to enhance.

With the Triennial Act that was passed,

Every three years the House would be asked,

To come together and explore,

Matters which Charles could not ignore.

No longer needing the king's approval,

Charles couldn't order their sudden removal.

A grasp at power by the Commons was meant,

And Charles was obliged to give his consent.

Then in March of that year, the trial began,

Of the Earl of Strafford, which only ran,

For just a few weeks, as the case fell apart,

The evidence suspect right from the start.

The leader of Parliament's powerful cause,

Was called John Pym, who worked without pause,

To see the Earl of Strafford incur,

Punishment and his name to slur.

So a bill of attainder was simply submitted,

With Strafford's sentence of death permitted,

If the king agreed to the death sentence,

Which Charles told Strafford would not gain acceptance.

But royalist officers attempted a coup,

With Charles involved, so Parliament knew,

There would be a public outcry,

So the Earl of Strafford had to die.

In May, Parliament issued their 'Protestation',

A petition filled with accusation,

Towards all those who did their best,

In making the nation feel oppressed.

All those who signed swore to defend,

Parliament, religion and to contend,

With those whose rule might be too hard,

But the honour of Charles they wouldn't discard.

For his and his family's life Charles feared,

As the image of losing it all appeared,

So Strafford's attainder was quickly signed,

His faithful ally now left behind.

Also in May, Charles had acceded,

Stating Parliament's voice must be heeded,

Before the House could be dissolved,

With the issue, at last, having evolved.

Charles and his Parliament seemed at last,

Having their differences behind them cast,

As now MP's were empowered, secure,

Wishing their status to last and endure.

Taxes which Parliament hadn't declared,

Were seen as unlawful and none were spared.

'Ship Money', which caused so much distress,

Was abolished as part of the MP's success.

John Pym and MP's had cause to relish,

The power they gained which would embellish,

Parliament and people, they represented,

As the rights of Parliament were reinvented.

Trouble in Ireland

A very old colony of the Normans first,

Ireland was, to England, cursed,

As most of the people there received,

Catholic sermons and were aggrieved.

For Ireland's people were very distinct,

Three different groups, but still somehow linked.

The Gaelic Irish were the oldest race,

While Norman English found its space.

Later came Protestant migration,

Keen to exploit the Irish nation.

Land for settlers was gradually taken,

Leaving the Catholics quiet and shaken.

But the three different groups lived in peace,

Though tension throughout would often increase,

As indigenous people saw their land given,

To settlers, while locals off land were driven.

It had always had its own Parliament,

And members to London's Parliament were sent,

To speak their minds and voice concern,

That the House might wish the facts to learn.

Yet the trouble in Ireland really started,

With steps on a path that was uncharted,

When the Earl of Strafford tried to endorse,

The use of an Irish Catholic force.

With a well-trained army at his back,

The king of England would not lack,

The power to induce and persuade,

That royal power must be obeyed.

But such a force only produced,

Unbalancing forces which were introduced,

Making the Irish Parliament aware,

Of growing tension they were quick to declare.

For Strafford had worked to confiscate,

Some Irish lands to satiate,

Protestant settler's selfish desire,

Cheap Irish lands to quickly acquire.

The Irish Parliament looked helpless and weak,

When a peaceful solution it had tried to seek.

But Strafford was working to further the aims,

Of Charles, his master, and help his claims.

With Strafford's impeachment, the three Irish factions,

Came closer together to focus their actions.

Each gave its evidence to help with the case,

Hoping they could his actions erase.

The Irish declared that they were still loyal,

To the king of England and all that was royal.

But the Catholic army that Strafford created,

Refused to disband as the English dictated.

Charles still kept the army together,

With the English Parliament wondering whether,

The king would use this Irish might,

To force his power and his right.

The lack of money would answer the question,

As the lack of pay lost Charles its possession,

With the Irish troops at last disbanding,

For want of funds, not Parliament's demanding.

Disputes over land quickly followed,

The Irish upset at demands they had swallowed.

For they were angry at the way it was handled,

Demanding the scheme should soon be dismantled.

The Irish Parliament was also upset,

With the way to side-line them in London was met.

They saw themselves as equal MP's,

Not London's servants to do with as they please.

The seeds of rebellion had now been sown,

The call for revenge on the settlers grown,

And when the Gaelic Irish struck,

Frustration and anger made them run amok.

It was October, sixteen forty-one,

And just as the killing had begun,

The old English in Ireland threw in their lot,

With the Gaelic Irish whose vengeance ran hot.

In the Commons, the rebels were seen,

As Catholic traitors whose acts were obscene.

Protestant settlers were brutally slain,

Subjected to torture, outrage and pain.

This was what the pamphlets said,

Which some in London quickly spread,

Leaving the nation full of desire,

To pour on the Irish Protestant fire.

Papist conspiracies circulated,

Horrible tales which were inflated.

Of Protestants murdered out of hand,

Even those who didn't make a stand.

Yet Charles was seen as slow and inept,

As the wave of fear over England swept.

He asked the Commons for funds to raise,

An army to end those rebellious ways.

But Parliament suspected and perceived,

That they, by Charles, might be deceived,

Believing he might then use that strength,

To reverse all setbacks he'd suffered at length.

Matters weren't helped when Charles was accused,

Of aiding those who killed and abused.

Rumours abounded that he was involved,

Explaining, they said, why it wasn't resolved.

The Commons suspected, and were afraid,

That if the plans for funds were laid,

To give the king a force to employ,

He'd use the force for their rights to destroy.

An army was needed to quickly deal,

With the Irish threat, which was very real,

As Protestants for the fight were braced,

Believing that Catholic intrigue was faced.

The Grand Remonstrance

By the end of the year, in November,

Parliament showed its mood and temper,

By taking a more belligerent stance,

Composing for Charles their Grand Remonstrance.

On December first, it was presented,

To the king who they resented,

For all the evils they had endured,

Yet still their loyalty was assured.

Much talk and anger was formulated,

By John Pym who was animated,

By what he believed had taken the nation,

To ruin, incompetence and stagnation.

Two hundred and four items were penned,

For Charles to read and comprehend,

Just how much the House was concerned,

How they, for sound rule, daily yearned.

Charles' rule was much criticised,

Though worded to show he wasn't despised,

But pointing the finger to others instead,

A Catholic influence which had spread.

Foreign, financial, religious and legal,

Policies showing his status so regal,

Were all attacked and soundly condemned,

But saying it wasn't from him that it stemmed.

Pym had struggled to get this through,

As many MP's rightly knew,

Charles wouldn't like what was included,

That affront to his majesty would be concluded.

Yet Pym pushed on, and the vote was taken,

Though he, and his followers, would be mistaken,

If they thought the document was to everyone's liking,

If they thought the effect on Charles would be striking.

The majority vote for the Bill was small,

By just eleven, but enough to call,

For the Grand Remonstrance to be permitted,

And have it all to Charles submitted.

But the document held more in store,

Attacking the king's reign at its core,

By demanding Bishops should be expelled,

With official appointments reduced, not swelled.

It also stated that Charles must show,

His acceptance that Parliament could always veto,

Anyone the king might choose to appoint,

To be an official and with power anoint.

It also focused on the Irish distress,

Which Parliament wanted to solve and redress,

That all land from rebels he'd confiscated,

Should not be sold or dissipated.

And in respect of their Lord and God,

The Remonstrance called for a general synod,

For likeminded Protestants to debate and pray,

Their God would show England the righteous way.

This was the document Parliament devised,

Hoping their grievance might be recognised,

By the king to whom all were serving,

But only if he was just and deserving.

An obscure MP named Oliver Cromwell,

Was delighted it passed, and a friend he'd tell,

That if it had failed, he was ready to leave,

For the New World, and for England grieve.

On the first of December, Charles was given,

The Grand Remonstrance, which throughout was riven,

With the points which Parliament had to deliver,

Though it left some MP's to fear and to shiver.

Charles took the document, and then delayed,

In giving the response for which many prayed.

So it was printed, and then it was shared,

With all of those who truly cared.

With the document out and disclosed,

The King's delay was quickly exposed.

But when, at last, he deemed to reply,

Most of the points he would seek to deny.

Stating that his overall impression,

Was nothing like his Parliament's expression,

And that, on the whole, he disagreed,

With points the Commons had said to take heed.

The seeds of mistrust began to run deeper,

With each side believing they were England's keeper.

The king saw in Parliament a definite threat,

Though open hostility hadn't come yet.

Pym was a Puritan who had been taught,

Law when young, so wouldn't be caught,

On any legal technicalities,

Or fear upsetting any formalities.

He was the King's greatest critic,

Intelligent, educated and analytic,

Believing the King was inclined,

Undisputed rule to find.

He knew that Charles would try to convince,

The nation that he was Lord and prince,

Ordained by God to rule alone,

The king's authority always known.

Preparations for War

In January, sixteen forty-two,

Tension in the nation grew,

As the struggle for power intensified,

With greater hostility identified.

For Charles took steps that were too drastic,

Desperate, severe and so fantastic,

That those in the Commons were agitated,

And anger with Charles was cultivated.

Then a critical point was reached,

With rumours Parliament would impeach,

The Queen, who was said to be conspiring,

With Irish rebels and their cause inspiring.

Charles then sent his troops to arrest,

Five of the House who'd done their best,

To try to steal his powers away,

Members of Parliament who'd had their say.

Pym, Hampden, Haselrig, Holles, Strode,

Those on which the wrath was bestowed,

Were to be held at Charles' discretion,

As part of Parliament's great suppression.

But word of the action reached them all,

Allowing the House to thwart and forestall,

An act which was seen as so aggressive,

And not, as Charles hoped, as impressive.

With the birds of the nest having flown,

The mask of a caring king was blown.

By trying to arrest five MP's,

The façade had fallen with greater ease.

The MP's had vanished, so Charles withdrew,

As a wave of anger in London blew.

Charles then left for Hampton Court,

Giving up London to the Commons' support

He'd also sent his Catholic queen,

To learn how events in Europe were seen,

Taking crown jewels to hopefully pawn,

Raising funds for when the swords were drawn.

And Parliament, not willing to give in at a whim,

In March a Bill was submitted by Pym,

Which would, it hoped, wrest control,

More power from Charles as a whole.

But the Militia Bill which Pym introduced,

Only greater hostility with Charles produced,

And the House of Lords were less than thrilled,

To see Pym's hostile plans fulfilled.

So the Commons had the Bill revised,

Into an ordinance and disguised,

Which meant the motion didn't need,

Neither King nor Lords to be agreed.

Pym and his followers tried to move,

An ordinance the Commons would approve,

Giving Parliament greater domination,

But causing trouble and aggravation.

In typical fashion, Charles had reacted,

With the issue getting more protracted,

And when the Tower of London was placed,

In his control it caused distaste.

Each side had struggled for ascendancy,

To rid themselves of dependency,

On anyone or anything,

Of House of Commons or privileged king.

Each, to the other, was a constant thorn,

Full of rhetoric and of scorn.

For years suspicion had been fed,

And only war could lie ahead.

Men on both sides would fight and revere,

The cause of dull Roundhead or bright Cavalier.

Men took up arms to fight a crusade,

For a different England to be made.

Yet still each side negotiated,

As men from both sides deliberated,

Believing, they thought, in clever speech,

That Reason might their hearts still reach.

Even as members of Parliament spoke,

Charles was plotting to break their yoke.

A cunning plan by him was hatched,

With him and his men to Hull dispatched.

The purpose of this covert mission,

Was seizing arms and ammunition,

Which would help the king to pledge,

That royal authority had an edge.

But Charles was about to have a surprise,

When the forces in Hull resisted his cries,

To hand the munitions over to him,

And gaining the edge soon looked very slim.

By the summer, both sides were arming,

With levels of distrust alarming.

Parliament saw Charles as arrogant, deceptive,

While he saw Parliament as unreceptive.

Then the Commons spoke and composed,

Nineteen Propositions which on Charles imposed,

A set of demands which were designed,

To have Charles' powers cut and confined.

By it, the Commons would have more sway,

In making decisions and be the mainstay,

Of England's rule and her policy,

In a fair and just democracy.

Charles rejected those propositions,

With a very firm admonition,

Rightly seeing that held within,

Were points that would his power unpin.

Using the age-old commission of array,

Charles now hoped to force his way,

By levying troops to force his opinion,

To defeat his foes and regain his dominion.

Parliament felt it had shed enough tears,

So summoned militias and keen volunteers,

To try to force their rights and their will,

On a king they'd fight but showed loyalty still.

With more negotiations rapidly failing,

And a mood of aggression now prevailing,

In August Charles decided to raise,

His standard and set the nation ablaze.

Gaining a port was now essential,

And Parliament saw the full potential,

Of capturing Portsmouth, which it obtained,

So vital supplies could be maintained.

Battle of Edgehill (Oct. 1642)

It was late in the year when war would commence,

When King and Parliament put aside pretence.

Yet many a man had already decided,

That England would fight and be divided.

Some sought God before they chose,

Before the spectre of war arose,

Praying that God would not conceal,

The side he blessed, and truth reveal.

Militias and veterans were collected,

That king and Parliament were protected,

From the other's act of aggression,

To fight the other's act of oppression.

The armies they raised were new and large,

Mostly unused to the battle's charge.

Yet they were filled with a righteous calling,

Ready, they thought, for war so appalling.

The king, at Shrewsbury, had made his base,

Then decided he would his enemies face,

So marched on London to bring about,

The blow to deliver a quick knockout.

Charles was confident in believing,

That battle would help him in retrieving,

His rights as king he thought were divine,

Restoring a rule he saw as benign.

Roundhead forces were commanded,

By the Earl of Essex, it being demanded,

That a man of experience and noble breeding,

Should lead the militia in fighting and bleeding.

The king was sure that if he stirred,

His threat to London boldly heard,

That Essex would not hesitate,

In meeting the threat and taking the bait.

It was late October when the armies met,

When the clash of wills would be set,

Near Edgehill in a Warwickshire field,

Determined to make the other yield.

Descending from their higher ground,

Advancing to the drummer's sound,

Royalists forces began the advance,

Taking the more aggressive stance.

Through his regiments Charles now rode,

To cheer his troops and Roundheads goad,

And seeing the king before them ride,

Parliament's anger could no more hide.

Cannon began to lob their shot,

As through his lines the king would trot,

Parliament hoping that one might find,

Its target if God were so inclined.

Charles thought better, and from harm departed,

As cannon fire from both sides started.

Yet even while the shot was exchanged,

A Royalist plan had been arranged.

The Royalist cavalry were duly sent,

To charge both wings and so prevent,

Parliament's forces from trying to turn,

The Royalist flank and victory earn.

For whoever managed to turn a flank,

Who, from the charge, never shrank,

Had a better chance to shatter,

The enemy's force, which might then scatter.

And the man to lead the Royalist charge,

Was a leader whose reputation was large.

Prince Rupert who to the king was related,

Whose cavalry skill was highly rated.

Some of the men who Rupert attacked,

Suddenly thought the wrong side had been backed,

Deciding they'd turn and join the king's side,

Leaving the rest of their troops mortified.

Soon the left flank of Parliament was lost,

Their cavalry beaten, and defences crossed.

But Rupert's cavalry continued pursuing,

Parliament's cavalry and their undoing.

The same had happened across the way,

With Parliament's right losing the fray.

Again the Royalist cavalry proceeded,

Pursuing their foe almost unimpeded.

The Royalist cavalry kept pushing on,

While cohesion broke, and their chance was gone,

To turn about and their charge to steer,

Into Parliament's infantry and its rear.

The Royalist infantry saw the flanks go,

Saw Parliament's left and right laid low,

So now advanced to what they thought,

Would be the enemy's infantry caught.

Much of Parliament's soldiery fled,

Having seen death and comrades who'd bled,

But some brigades still held firm,

As they watched the others run and squirm.

Then through their ranks horsemen appeared,

Cavalry who'd rallied and seemed not affeared,

As toward the Royalist lines they surged,

As cavalry and infantry together merged.

The Royalist cavalry were still out raiding,

In Parliament's rear as the day was fading.

Intent on looting the baggage train,

Rupert could not make his troopers abstain.

Charles had also failed to conserve,

His own lifeguards as strategic reserve,

Allowing his troopers to take their part,

In Rupert's charge which had won at the start.

And while they watched the cavalry dashing,

Towards the flanks with sword blades flashing,

Now the king wished he'd kept them nearer,

As the Roundhead threat was getting clearer.

The Royalist infantry fought in vain,

As Parliament's forces they couldn't contain.

Then, when the Royalist centre crumbled,

Charles, and his men, were greatly humbled.

Reaching the king's artillery positions,

Dispersing men and destroying munitions,

The cavalry decided it was best to withdraw,

Leaving the Royalists bloodied and raw.

By now the Royalist horse were returning,

And both sides were clearly yearning,

For darkness to mark the battle's end,

And further fighting to suspend.

Troops who found themselves dispersed,

Who fear and wounds now painfully nursed,

Trudged in the dark to find their brigade,

The trauma of battle leaving many dismayed.

At the end of the day, both sides had retreated,

Their decisive victory not being completed.

Both would take stock, and were compelled,

To think of what this battle spelled.

Shortly thereafter, at Turnham Green,

They met, but battle wasn't seen,

As both sides stood, watched and stared,

No bloody charge being dared.

It was late in the year, So Charles decided,

To withdraw to Oxford which provided,

An ideal city that would operate,

As the base on which to concentrate.

They had to re-think their strategy,

If they hoped to end this tragedy,

Where Englishmen fought and killed each other,

Father against son, brother against brother.

Skirmishes, Victories & Defeats

(Nov. 1642-August 1643)

Edgehill left many feeling shocked,

By the blood and death when horns were locked,

But still the issue could not be evaded,

With attacks on each other being traded.

Late in the year, Brentford was taken,

By Rupert's forces leaving Parliament shaken.

But then Prince Rupert was confronted,

By larger forces, his progress was blunted.

The Prince had thought to take his force,

To London itself, and attack the source,

Where open rebellion to Charles had sprouted,

Hoping, no doubt, it would be routed.

But Rupert was forced to quickly retire,

When a larger foe forced his plan to expire.

He knew that to ask his troops to stand,

Would end in defeat as Parliament planned.

Everywhere seemed to be getting embroiled,

In a conflict which through counties uncoiled.

Each was intent to recruit through each shire,

To recruit every farmhand, noble or squire.

In January, sixteen forty-three,

Charles was happy to finally see,

Success at Nantwich and Braddock Down,

Steps on the road to taking each town.

Yet, Parliament also enjoyed its success,

Adding to their own progress,

When Lichfield, Wakefield and Reading fell,

To Roundhead attacks and their pious yell.

Back and forth the armies went,

Marching for miles until they were spent,

Sometimes facing stiff opposition,

Or easily changing the foe's disposition.

To each the towns and cities were falling,

Taken then lost in the see saw brawling.

Then Cavaliers, with sword and pistol,

Took the vital city and port of Bristol.

With this in their hands, they could receive,

Help from abroad, and might yet achieve,

Ultimate victory with foreign assistance,

Ensuring a long and defiant resistance.

But in June the struggle became intense,

When a Royalist force which was immense,

Marched through Yorkshire to capture a city,

To defeat the Roundheads without pity.

Bradford was the target in mind,

The Earl of Newcastle the general assigned,

To defeat the Roundheads and claim the north,

Making a stronghold for Charles thenceforth.

General Fairfax was Parliament's man,

Knowing his force would have to ban,

The Royalist progress, and had to choose,

To face a siege or a battle lose.

Fairfax marched and chose to avoid,

A siege so his troops could be better employed.

Meeting the Foe at Adwalton Moor,

He knew that his chances of winning were poor.

For ten thousand Royalists had already formed,

The four thousand Roundheads position stormed.

It looked like the Roundheads might yet prevail,

But hopes of victory soon turned stale.

For Royalist numbers eventually told,

Despite the Roundhead attack so bold.

Fairfax and his men were depleted,

And the Royalist hold in the north was completed.

In the north, for Parliament, Hull remained,

With Royalist power unrestrained.

Something drastic would need to be done,

To put an end to the Royalist run.

So Parliament entered negotiations,

That would create such strong foundations,

To the cause against their king,

Which would their ultimate victory bring.

Scotland, by Charles, was alienated,

When to their kirk he had dictated,

That they should worship as he prescribed,

Should follow the worship he described.

They'd fought a war for liberation,

From what they saw as desecration,

Of their kirk they held as sacred,

And interference, so blunt and naked.

Puritan church and Scottish kirk,

Would not their similar objectives shirk,

Forming an alliance to work as one,

Until their king was at last outdone.

This Solemn League and Covenant,

Signed by those of each government,

Was signed in August, promising to protect,

Church and kirk, and rights to respect.

But a war with Charles still had to proceed,

With little sign he would concede.

Still the blood would have to be let,

Before a righteous rule was set.

In the south, the fighting continued,

With bloody engagements often viewed,

When Roundhead met with Cavalier,

Attacking when their troops were near.

When forces crossed each other's path,

Near Devizes or important Bath,

Shots were fired and swords were wielded,

As forces on both sides were fielded.

Counties which were far removed,

From the beginning quickly proved,

They could raise a force to support,

The cause and outcome which they sought.

Local men from town and village,

Fearing those who sought to pillage,

The land and houses which they held,

Fought that foes might be expelled.

But many were not drilled or versed,

To deal with that which on them burst,

Leaving many shocked and broken,

Undisciplined troops afraid, outspoken.

Across the country, fighting crept,

Unrelenting, it never slept,

As causes struggled to persuade,

Each town and borough to give its aid.

In time the county men were pressed,

Taken from homes to do their best,

To fight in a cause that wasn't theirs,

To kill and die for other's cares.

Experienced men or frightened boys,

All exposed to the battle's noise.

Facing the same dangers alike,

Taught to handle musket and pike.

First Battle of Newbury (Sept. 1643)

For Charles it was a successful year,

With Roundhead losing to Cavalier.

Banbury, Oxford and Reading fell,

Along with important Bristol as well.

With the city of Bristol in Royalist hands,

Charles was confident to retrieve those lands,

Which were under Parliament's control,

Which he believed the rebels stole.

He journeyed to Bristol to congratulate,

Prince Rupert's success and administrate,

A strategic plan that might bear fruit,

And destroy his enemies at the root.

The Royalist western army stayed,

In Dorset and Cornwall to fight and dissuade,

Their foe from moving, leaving many shaken,

With the key town of Dorchester being taken.

Even Parliament's Eastern Association,

That Roundhead rich and strong creation,

Saw its plans disintegrate,

But not too much to annihilate.

Essex, Hertfordshire and Norfolk,

Cambridgeshire and also Suffolk,

Later joined by Huntingdonshire,

Then by the county of Lincolnshire.

These were the counties who could afford,

To equip their militias with musket and sword,

Then keeping their troops well provisioned,

Though the length of the war was not envisioned.

Formed by counties that weren't so poor,

It meant that they could build a core,

Of men who had much better supplies,

Better equipment to galvanise.

But at Gainsborough and Winceby too,

The hope of defeating Royalists flew,

When the army was soundly beaten,

And confident words had to be eaten.

Along with all the Royalist success,

Parliament's cause looked like a mess,

With Charles then proceeding on to Gloucester,

Which would more fear in Parliament foster.

So the Earl of Essex was forced to raise,

An ad hoc army to halt this phase,

Of Royalist victories which, it seemed,

Was just as Charles had planned and dreamed.

At Gloucester, the Royalists had a surprise,

When Essex appeared before their eyes,

Using his army to force a break,

Of the city's siege, which Charles hoped to take.

But Essex himself was also required,

To retreat to London before he was mired,

In a battle he knew he might well lose,

So chose instead the fight to refuse.

Yet the Royalist army knew where he'd go,

And Essex and his troops were slow,

Which helped the Royalists, who were adept,

In moving faster to intercept.

At Newbury Essex found his path barred,

So his plan to retreat he'd have to discard,

Knowing he'd have to turn and face,

The Royalist army or suffer disgrace.

Essex attacked in the early morning,

Just as the autumn day was dawning,

Pushing the Royalists off the high ground,

Positions the Royalists thought were sound.

Yet the Cavalier troops were undeterred,

With the thought of victory well ensured,

So into the Roundhead lines they went,

Their anger and fury to purge and vent.

Losses were heavy, but not in vain,

As Parliament's forces felt the strain,

Until a central hill was seized,

And with-it Royalist worries eased.

Parliament's centre was almost surrounded,

As the line was attacked and constantly pounded,

But Essex reacted, and the troops were rallied,

Though the Royalist position wasn't carried.

Parliament's counterattack was slowed,

As Royalist superiority showed.

Slowly retiring, Essex instructed,

His reserve to the front be conducted.

But this force itself was set upon,

An attack which broke their echelon,

And the longed for help then retreated,

Leaving Parliament's centre depleted.

Parliament's line was soon split in two,

Their hope of winning gone askew,

With Cavalier forces hoping to press,

An attack in the centre to complete the mess.

But the Royalist forces had to engage,

A force whose ability they couldn't gauge,

Men from London's parish and borough,

Whose zeal and loyalty were very thorough.

Trained London Bands stopped the progression,

But the gloom of night stopped their procession,

Putting an end to another day's fighting,

Horrid to some, to others exciting.

Each side was forced to then attend,

To the cost in terms of foe and friend.

The wounded and dying needed care,

By men exhausted, with nothing to spare.

Parliament's forces had been saved,

By dark and the way the Bands behaved.

Both had arrived in the nick of time,

Halting the Royalist's victorious climb.

Next morning, Parliament's men presumed,

That more of the fighting would be resumed,

Believing they'd face more of the same,

More death and glory in Parliament's name.

Yet the Royalist position was also dire,

Lack of munitions forcing them to retire.

The Royalist army was forced to drag,

Itself from the victory they had in the bag.

Departing Royalists were the guarantee,

That Essex and his army were now free,

To retreat to London as he'd proposed,

Knowing, for now, he was unopposed.

Battle of Marston Moor (June 1644)

Prelude

Late in sixteen forty-three,

The king believed he'd found the key,

To ending the war in his favour,

Convincing his council he'd never waver.

For Charles had secretly negotiated,

A deal with the Irish he'd cultivated,

Which meant the trouble in Ireland ended,

With the role of the army their suspended.

Regiments could flock to help the king,

Defeat his Parliament and hopefully bring,

An end to the war, which was growing,

Bitter and long with no end to it showing.

Yet Parliament's plans had soon responded,

When Scotland's Parliament, with whom they'd bonded,

Sent troops to England to lend support,

That together their king might be fought.

In early sixteen forty-four,

The Scottish army, who loyalty swore,

Marched south to crush the Royalist cause,

To Roundhead approval and great applause.

The Royalist forces were besieging Hull,

But their time in the north became less dull,

By the presence of those Scottish forces,

An army of men, guns and horses.

The Earl of Leven led the Scots,

A veteran general who'd faced the shots,

In Europe's wars of religious hate,

Now leading his country's forces by fate.

The Marquess of Newcastle led the king's men,

Not knowing how, where or when,

The Scots would attack, so he had to take stock,

Of how he could this invading force block.

The Royalist force was then divided,

With enough for the siege of Hull provided,

While Newcastle took what forces he had,

To make the Scottish advance go bad.

The Marquess of Newcastle moved his line,

To prevent the foe from crossing the Tyne,

For if it was crossed, the defence would break,

And could the city of Newcastle take.

In April, a Parliament force approached,

Nearer to Hull where the siege encroached,

Forcing the Royalist commander to act,

For fear his siege might be cracked.

Moving to Selby, the Royalists prepared,

To meet the Roundheads if battle was dared.

But the Royalist stronghold of Selby was stormed,

With the Marquess of its defeat informed.

The Marquess now realised York was at risk,

With Roundhead actions in the north being brisk.

York was a major Royalist centre,

Which he knew the Roundheads mustn't enter.

But the siege of York soon commenced,

Leaving Charles and his council so incensed,

That this major bastion of Royalist power,

Would be subjected to the enemy's glower.

And as the siege of York proceeded,

Other moves by Roundheads would be needed,

As smaller Royalist towns were taken,

Leaving Royalist power in the north forsaken.

The Eastern Association sent,

An army in June to help prevent,

Any Royalist moves they chose to make,

Knowing exactly what was at stake.

Troops of three armies had converged,

Besieging York and together merged,

Into one force so the siege was sealed,

With the strength of their purpose so revealed.

They knew the Royalists would seek York's relief,

So they quickly elected a commander in chief,

Choosing the Earl of Leven to be,

Their leader as none had experience like he.

The Roundheads knew there was little doubt,

That a Royalist force would soon set out,

To come to the city's urgent aid,

And hopes for reconquest wouldn't fade.

Prince Rupert was chosen as the best,

Who, with skill, had been blessed.

An experienced fighter who was resolved,

About whose person élan revolved.

Prince Rupert had an arduous task,

One which no élan could mask,

For he would face a force combined,

In religion and politics so aligned.

Rupert's forces duly proceeded,

On their march and had succeeded,

In gathering troops and also defeating,

Parliament's forces, but success was fleeting.

Then the prince had a letter and was advised,

Of Charles's position, and was surprised,

How the king requested York be relieved,

But also of a different plan then conceived.

For Charles had been forced to leave Oxford fast,

When a Roundhead force upon him was cast,

And Charles now asked the Prince to step in,

Taking York and aid for Charles to begin.

With an army of fourteen thousand strong,

Rupert proceeded, and it wasn't long,

Before he was just fourteen miles away,

At Knaresborough Castle where he would stay.

The Earl of Leven had recognised,

His army's positions were compromised,

If Rupert should suddenly decide to engage,

And an outright battle decide to wage.

So, at the end of June, the siege was raised,

With those in York relieved and amazed.

For Leven decided to concentrate,

His army before it was far too late.

Leven advanced to block Rupert's approach,

So that Rupert could not on York encroach.

With a much larger army, he felt secure,

To block the Royalists at Marston Moor.

The Battle

Whilst Leven's army was deployed,

He and his generals were annoyed,

To hear of Rupert's daring stride,

Which reached York and those inside.

A bridge across the river Ouse,

Which Leven's forces needed to use,

Had been taken, and was barred,

Which Royalist troops planned to guard.

The Roundhead forces rightly feared,

That a path to their supplies was cleared,

Which, they thought, the Prince would pursue,

And would to the Royalist cause accrue.

Yet Rupert had been clearly instructed,

That help for the king should not be obstructed,

With Parliament's northern force to be crushed,

That help to the king could be rushed.

So Rupert returned to face his rival,

Giving Leven's hopes a keen revival,

That he might have, at last, a chance,

To knock Prince Rupert's plans askance.

But the Marquess of Newcastle was opposed,

To any pitch battle the foe composed,

Telling the Prince that he was worried,

This attack was all too hurried.

The Marquess asked and implored,

To wait for more troops, but was ignored,

As the Prince was sure what he had to do,

And so to chance his gauntlet threw.

With twenty-two thousand men arrayed,

Coalition forces were displayed.

Rupert had seventeen thousand or so,

Who hoped they could their bravery show.

The Scottish and English coalition,

Were on higher ground and in addition,

Had more troops and cannon to utilise,

Of which their success would comprise.

Royalist cavalry advanced and yearned,

To take a position that a flank might be turned,

But this turned into a wasted ride,

When defeated by Cromwell's Ironsides.

This was the man who'd thought of leaving,

His native country whilst perceiving,

That England's plight was becoming a curse,

Corrupt, unfair and getting worse.

But when the Remonstrance was delivered,

Cromwell's plans of leaving withered.

So, in the war he was committed,

Fighting that parliament be acquitted.

Yet time had passed, and it was too late,

To start any action to decide their fate,

So Royalist forces were given permission,

To settle and rest from their commission.

The Earl of Leven had taken note,

Saw his chance to take them by the throat,

And ordered his regiments to prepare,

To advance to catch their foe in the snare.

It was late in the day when shots were exchanged,

When the last dispositions were arranged.

A Summer's evening in early July,

When cannon balls began to fly,

Cavalry waited on every wing,

Who hoped to the mass of infantry bring,

Success on the day by turning a flank,

To clear the path for the infantry's rank.

Over the moor, a thunderstorm broke,

The darkening skies beginning to cloak,

The regiments that were getting nearer,

And Leven's plan growing clearer.

The Royalist right was swiftly driven,

By Roundhead infantry when battle was given,

Turning the line and making it creak,

A Royalist brigade whose ranks became weak.

The Royalist right would also meet,

A cavalry charge from Cromwell's elite.

Royalist troops had Ironsides to face,

Had a mighty charge to hopefully brace.

In a bitter fight, Cromwell was grazed,

Wounded by shot and slightly dazed,

But his disciplined troops carried on,

When he, to the rear, for care had gone.

Seeing his right was beginning to crumble,

And fearing the troops and leader might stumble,

Rupert became very aware,

He'd need to lead his cavalry there.

Into the charge his troopers sped,

Ignoring the wounded and the dead,

Hoping that the flank could be saved,

And a path to victory could be paved.

By now their leader, Cromwell, was back,

Leading his men once more in attack,

Facing what Rupert's troops had to give,

To see whose grasp at victory would live.

Charged in the flank and at the front,

Rupert's men tried to blunt,

Cromwell's men who refused to quit,

As they stabbed, slashed, shot and hit.

Hacking each other with the sword's edge,

Squeezed together in line or wedge,

Ironsides cut and were cut as well,

But Cromwell's discipline was beginning to tell.

They stood their ground despite the strain,

Of Rupert's elite and the blood and the pain,

Until Scottish infantry tipped the scale,

Proving to Rupert his attempt would fail.

Coming to Cromwell's urgent aid,

Success on the right at last was made,

With Rupert's elite quickly scattered,

Dreams of winning rapidly shattered.

The sounds of men who sought to be brave,

Hoping their courage would spare them the grave,

Yelling and shouting as regiments closed,

Seeing the danger their enemy posed.

A man would see his comrades fall,

A moment ago, seen standing tall,

Then laid out by the unseen shot,

Forever still on his bloody spot.

Units walked on through the smoke,

The acrid fumes making men choke,

Until, at last, they could easily spy,

The foe in front who would have to die.

After inaccurate shots were exchanged,

The method of war was not unchanged,

With blades coming out to stab and slice,

A thrust to the throat making death precise.

The battle devolved to personal combat,

Ancient, brutal and proving that,

The business of war hadn't changed much,

Relying on men in a deadly clutch.

Such personal fights could become fierce,

Stabbing and thrusting hoping to pierce,

An enemy's soft and vulnerable flesh,

With the smell of blood forever fresh.

At last the Royalist right was routed,

Coalition victory now undoubted,

As Rupert and his men were pursued,

Their aggressive spirit now subdued.

Yet the coalition right had failed,

Its attempt at winning badly derailed,

With Royalist forces there elated,

That the enemy's plan was frustrated.

With horse and foot working together,

For a time it seemed doubtful whether,

The coalition army would win,

As their lines on the right began to wear thin.

Roundheads ran without firing a shot,

With panic adding to the rot,

Of regiments which just wanted to leave,

To go to the rear and safety retrieve.

Most of the troops had little skill,

In using their weapons whilst trying to kill.

Most relied on God and luck,

Desperately trying not to be struck.

For many, the fear was just too immense,

The noise and fear too intense,

And so they decided they had to admit,

It was time to leave and their soldiering quit.

Those who stayed might fall with a groan,

Broken bodies lying prone,

Numbed by the blow and the shock,

Felled by the strike they failed to block.

In time, the pain of wounds so bad,

Could drive strong men almost mad,

As wounded men soon comprehended,

Their pain and fears they apprehended.

Some might be found and then removed,

Back to the rear, but things rarely improved,

For medicine then could barely cope,

Leaving surgeons to painfully probe and grope.

Wounds that were treated or barely inspected,

There was always a fear they'd become infected.

Veterans knew the gangrenous smell,

Delivering pain and its own special hell.

Shattered limbs would be amputated,

But pain and risk weren't alleviated.

The victim would be held and restrained,

Biting on straps so shrieks were contained.

Instant death to a wound was preferred,

Not the painful end which was deferred.

Comrades would pray for their friends to heal,

But God ignored their zealous appeal.

Soon the path was open to the baggage train,

Where Royalists headed and whose goal was plain.

Here they'd find much wealth to loot,

More intent on plunder than foes to shoot.

It was then that Cromwell's disciplined force,

Helped to turn the battle's course,

When he and his men returned to the fight,

To stop the coalition's plight.

Hitting the Royalists hard and swift,

His heavy cavalry giving short shrift,

He caught his enemy unawares,

Who gazed upon him with frightened stares.

For this attack was unexpected,

Against the foe who had collected,

To loot and thought they'd cause to cheer,

Not expecting the cavalry to reappear.

The Royalist troops were disorganised,

Tired after getting the loot which they prized,

To offer resistance that was effective,

Their exhaustion making defence defective.

Yet many were rallied and then would turn,

To face the charge but they would learn,

The effect of a force which was well trained,

Which helped the attack to be sustained.

When the charge upon them came,

Many just ran to their shame,

Refusing to fight despite the urging,

Fearful of where the foe was surging.

The coalition was free to tender,

To where the enemy's will was slender,

Where resistance there looked very defiant,

Who, for quarter, would not be suppliant.

The cavalry charged, and Royalists died,

Even those who fleeing tried.

Fugitives ran, but horsemen chased,

Terrified men in death debased.

All that was left were those who stood,

Proud, defiant and a brotherhood,

Of men who to their king were loyal,

Brave defenders of his power so royal.

Yet a wall of flesh could not stop,

Overwhelming force, and they would drop,

Until just thirty stood unwavering,

Surrendering when fate was so unfavouring.

The Royalist loss had been emphatic,

Its consequence for Charles dramatic.

Much Royalist blood had been spilled,

With about four thousand of them killed.

The day's events were indelibly etched,

On mind and body fully stretched,

Leaving the men shaken and numb,

Exhausted, thoughtful and strangely dumb.

Not long after, York surrendered,

A major bastion to Parliament rendered.

The Royalist stronghold had to accept,

That a good defence couldn't be kept.

The Royalist threat in the north was removed,

And Parliament's position had improved.

Cromwell had shown what discipline meant,

When time and effort on training was spent.

With the Royalist threat in the north decreased,

The Eastern Association was released,

To move further south in operations,

To help with Parliament's aspirations.

Second Battle of Newbury (Oct. 1644)

In the south, the king still worked hard,

That Parliament's forces there be barred,

From gaining towns and communities,

Pursuing chances and opportunities.

Parliament's force led by Waller and Essex,

Had made much progress in the region of Wessex,

Marching on Oxford, forcing Charles to run,

Who moved by night to avoid the June sun.

But while at Worcester, Charles had learnt,

The forces of Waller and Essex weren't,

Working as one, and had divided,

Leaving Charles free for the plan he decided.

Essex had gone to help relieve,

Lyme Regis in Dorset, leaving Charles to deceive,

Waller who was left behind,

To follow Charles and his army to find.

But Charles had slipped past Waller's spies,

Returning to Oxford for more men and supplies,

Then at Cropredy Bridge Charles inflicted,

Defeat on Waller as he had predicted.

The king was free to pursue and hunt,

The army of Essex and its leader confront.

But Essex withdrew to Lostwithiel in Cornwall,

Allowing the king his siege to install.

Essex abandoned his troops to their fate,

Leaving the port before it was too late.

Charles was free to probe and scout,

And Parliament's strength in the south to flout.

The defence of Plymouth by Charles was tested,

But the king turned away in case he was bested.

He marched through the south helping those under siege,

With towns giving thanks to their master and liege.

Soon he was joined by Rupert who told,

How his army could not the enemy hold,

And how at Marston he was subdued,

But not by his bravery or ineptitude.

By now the armies of Parliament drew near,

Their plan to face Charles being quite clear.

So Charles sent Rupert with a force to distract,

That the Prince might some of that force attract.

But the Earl of Essex, who was back in the field,

Would not fall for the bait that appealed,

But kept his forces together instead,

As together they'd fill the foe with dread.

For Essex had his and Waller's troops,

The remnants who'd made it back in groups,

But the Eastern Association also was there,

Under the Earl of Manchester's care.

It was late October by the time Charles had,

Saved Donnington Castle, where the siege was bad.

He hoped Basing House would be saved by him soon,

But the presence of Essex denied him this boon.

So Charles decided to wait at Newbury,

Now his plans were going to the contrary.

He hoped for Rupert and his men to return,

As large enemy forces gave Charles great concern.

Royalist forces were greatly surpassed,

By Parliament's army approaching fast.

Charles would have to rely on defence,

To stop and contain the foe so immense.

Donnington Castle, Shaw House, the village of Speen,

Were quickly identified by Charles and seen,

As places where a defence could be made,

Where his troops might stand and blows then trade.

The Kennet and Lambourn rivers might assist,

His regiments of men to resist,

The brutal assault he knew would fall,

As Parliament tried to attack and maul.

Charles kept his cavalry in reserve,

To use if his troops broke the foe's nerve.

With men in position, all they could do,

Was wait 'til the foe upon them drew.

On the twenty sixth of October,

Parliament's forces drew ever closer,

Approaching the enemy lines to inspect,

To see any weakness they might detect.

Clay Hill, near Newbury, was occupied,

By Roundhead cannon and shots were tried,

To see what damage could be wrought,

If any alarm to the foe might be brought.

Also Waller marched several miles,

With twelve thousand men in columns and files,

To fall on Speen from the west,

Outflanking Royalists, and defences to test.

The move on Speen was soon detected,

Its move to outflank being suspected,

But though the king was not surprised,

The troops who were there weren't advised.

At three o'clock in the afternoon,

Roundhead forces were assembled and strewn,

Before the village, and the attack commenced,

Against Royalist forces, surprised and incensed.

Cromwell, with cavalry, was on the left,

This force under him proving quick and deft,

In the centre was Skippon with those on foot,

Balfour on the right with more mounted input.

Prince Maurice, Rupert's brother from the Rhine,

Commanded the Royalist battle line,

That Waller was hoping to assault and breach,

Intending the village of Speen to reach.

Royalist troops had been dispersed,

Foraging wide when upon them burst,

The foot and horse which Waller had formed,

And which upon their line had stormed.

The Royalists put up a stiff resistance,

But with Waller and his troops' persistence,

Forced their way into the village,

But not without pain and blood's great spillage.

Balfour's cavalry had mainly enjoyed,

Success until there was deployed,

The Queen's Regiment of foot and horse,

Which almost altered the battle's course.

For a while, Parliament's right was checked,

The charge on the flank looking wrecked.

Cromwell's move into action was also slow,

And forced to retreat by the Royalist flow.

But the attack on Speen had a culmination,

When Parliament's might and determination,

Forced Royalist troops to at last vacate,

And Parliament's will to at last placate.

Manchester also led a diversion,

Attacking Shaw House to make an incursion,

Into the Royalist fortifications,

Having hopeful expectations.

Supposed to work in coordination,

Parliament's attack knew frustration,

When Manchester failed to hear his cue,

When Waller's guns on the village drew.

The attack on Shaw house went in late,

Failed and meant the plan would stagnate,

Meaning that Parliament couldn't displace,

The Royalist defence from its base.

With darkness came the usual switch,

To relative quiet from battle's pitch,

As troops decided enough was enough,

And Parliament knew they'd had a rebuff.

Though defence of Shaw House had not been dashed,

The Royalist lines there had not crashed,

Charles and his generals rightly assumed,

That their defence could not be resumed.

Greatly outnumbered and outgunned,

Further action by Charles was shunned.

Instead, they withdrew at first light,

Believing the move to be wise and right.

Their path to Oxford wasn't blocked,

Their rear-guard not by the enemy knocked.

When Parliament's cavalry finally rode,

Charles crossed the mighty Thames which flowed.

Turning to Donnington Castle instead,

Parliament's force around it spread,

But the attack they made was delivered with haste,

With many killed in attacks so misplaced.

Then on the first day of November,

In Oxford, which was the king's nerve centre,

Rupert arrived and the king's army swelled,

And Royalist fears were quickly quelled.

On the ninth of November, they went to relieve,

Donnington Castle and its force to reprieve,

From Parliament's army who stood all around,

Whose noise from the guns off the wall would resound.

But when the army of Charles was observed,

The Earl of Manchester was reserved,

In offering battle, and decided to choose,

Retreat, and no battle he feared he'd lose.

By the nineteenth, Basing House too,

Flags of royal loyalty flew.

Parliament's army leaders had showed,

How the presence of Charles could spirits erode.

For the presence of Charles was sufficient,

To make Parliament's generals less proficient,

Filling their hearts and minds with distress,

An urge to submit it was hard to suppress.

For the Roundhead army suffered division,

Divided in policy, plan and decision.

Whenever the leaders had conferred,

Their ultimate goal was always blurred.

Manchester knew that whenever they fought,

If they lost just once, they could be brought,

Down to their knees and Charles would bring,

Death upon them for fighting their king.

Cromwell could see just what this meant,

Believing that they, by God, were sent,

To take up arms and tyranny erase,

Or to make peace, 'be it never so base'.

Cromwell and others like him expressed,

Their dissatisfaction and weren't impressed,

By the way that Parliament's army was led,

And moved to deprive it of its head.

Battle of Naseby (June 1645)

Prelude

In late November, sixteen forty-four,

As the conflict progressed ever more,

There were those who served and identified,

Where their cause would slowly slide.

They saw the army and leadership,

Caught in the past's traditional grip,

With lords and high-born men commanding,

Given rank by their noble standing.

They felt the struggle was also lacking,

The total commitment and the backing,

Of peers who could not really discern,

From the old ways, of which they would yearn.

Some of Parliament's righteous core,

Did not hold the king in awe,

But saw in Charles the evil root,

That had begun this fierce dispute.

These men of Parliament saw the need,

For change and how they must proceed,

In making war with a force so new,

It would for them see this struggle through.

When the Eastern Association stated,

Its funds for proceeding were deflated,

Parliament saw they would have to be prompt,

Or else with disaster they'd be swamped.

The Committee of Both Kingdoms was constructed,

That Scotland and England might be instructed,

On how the war was being pursued,

And to help both Parliament's win this feud.

Now they were asked to write a report,

To appeal to the Commons for their support,

In making a new and radical change,

And help their position to rearrange.

On the nineteenth of December,

Parliament asked every member,

To vote for the Self-Denying Act,

Which caused the peers to loudly react.

For the Act, when passed, had the mission,

Of excluding those who held a commission,

From serving in Parliament and the army too,

To choose one or the other as interests blew.

It was aimed at the leaders of Parliament's defence,

Who'd shown lack of spirit at the army's expense.

Leaders like Manchester, Essex and Waller as well,

Lost their positions, and from command fell.

On January sixth, sixteen forty-five,

A new creation became alive,

In the seeds of an army which were implanted,

To grow and succeed that victory be granted.

All through winter and early spring,

Each day of training would closer bring,

A greater hope that they would attain,

Success in the field and the Royalists constrain.

The army would be a professional core,

Which Parliament's hope for the future bore.

Men who as regular soldiers were paid,

Trained and disciplined, not showing they're afraid.

Two shillings for cavalry troopers each day,

Eight pence for infantry come what may.

Food and clothing were greatly improved,

Which those at the bottom greatly approved.

Pious and disciplined, they would seek,

Fitness for war and healthier physique,

In putting aside all things from their camp,

That might of immorality stamp.

The New Model Army adopted a code,

That demonstrated their fighting mode.

Led by men through whom they believed,

Their ultimate victory might be achieved.

With a tough discipline from the start,

Troops were taught the soldier's art.

A man could be punished, as word soon spread,

For just calling a comrade another Roundhead.

On paper the army now consisted,

Of twenty-two thousand who were enlisted.

Twenty-three regiments of foot and horse,

Parliament's army and its winning source.

But some of the men had been afflicted,

By being those who were conscripted,

So when the army marched in May,

Four thousand or so had gone astray.

Yet those who stayed and chose to remain,

Were professional troops and not militia again.

These were better than those before,

A force the Royalists could not ignore.

No longer would leaders be chosen or picked,

Because they were noble in a code that was strict,

Taking command because of their birth,

But were chosen to lead because of their worth.

By April, the army was good to proceed,

To where its leader saw the need.

And those in Parliament were impressed,

By the man to whom command was blessed.

Sir Thomas Fairfax had been selected,

When his skill in battle was detected.

As Captain General he was appointed,

By Parliament and their God anointed.

The Self-Denying Ordinance became law,

And many left the army, but Fairfax saw,

A quality in one that would always tell,

A colonel of horse named Oliver Cromwell.

Fairfax gave Cromwell his cavalry command,

As he had shown his tactics were grand.

To the Self-Denying Act an exception was made,

That Cromwell, once more, might use his blade.

Yet while the New Model Army prepared,

Whilst faults in leadership were repaired,

Charles had made Prince Rupert his chief,

To end the war to the king's relief.

At the start of May, Rupert recommended,

Attacks on the foe should not be suspended,

Putting forward a plan to help retake,

The north of England in victory's wake.

Yet other advisers of Charles also said,

If attacks on the New Model Army were led,

Then Parliament's force would not be reduced,

But Charles, by Rupert's plan, was seduced.

So Charles then left with his army to crush,

Parliament's hold in the north and to rush,

That with Scottish Royalists he might meet,

And the reconquest of the north to complete.

Charles was forced to keep some troops back,

That the siege of Taunton he might crack,

But the New Model Army turned its attention,

To the city of Oxford, with the king's apprehension.

Oxford was Charles' wartime base,

His capital city where court took place,

So to lose it to Parliament would be a shock,

Might victory for the Roundheads unlock.

Seeing the danger, the king reacted,

Believing the enemy must be distracted,

Knowing he'd have a move to perform,

So took the city of Leicester by storm.

Oxford was struggling as provisions were low,

With the Royalist garrison unable to know,

If they could survive a concerted assault,

Whether the troops would fight or bolt.

Parliament reasoned that the major threat,

Was the king's army which they couldn't forget,

As it roamed the north hardly contested,

With Parliament's towns and cities molested.

So Fairfax decided to leave Oxford alone,

The taking of Oxford to postpone,

And head to the north so he could track,

Royalist forces and their mettle crack.

But Charles was already heading his way,

To help relieve Oxford and its dismay.

On the thirteenth of June, first contact was struck,

Near the village of Naseby by chance and potluck.

The Battle

On the fourteenth, men were readied,

The fearful rallied, and nerves were steadied,

As the foggy dawn began to grow lighter,

Fate awaiting every fighter.

The Royalist line, a mile and a half long,

Was, they thought, somewhat strong.

Though greatly outnumbered, their king was nearby,

So each, for their king, their best would try.

Their infantry centre was well constructed,

And under Lord Astley would be conducted,

Into the battle and shortly to close,

With Parliament's waiting infantry rows.

With Royalist cavalry placed on each wing,

Keen to attack and the battle to swing,

Rupert and his brother were on the right flank,

While the left had Langdale's cavalry rank.

The New Model Army was drawn up on a crest,

A mile north of Naseby and properly dressed,

Skippon had the centre with men on foot,

While cavalry on the wings were put.

Ireton's cavalry on the left were prepared,

To charge and across the battlefield stared,

Whilst on the right, Cromwell stood,

His regiments placed as best they could.

Yet Fairfax had kept some troops obscured,

Behind the crest and well secured,

Away from Charles and his army's sight,

Which helped the Royalist hopes to ignite.

For Charles and his generals were deceived,

By the enemy force which they perceived.

All were arrayed and waiting to start,

The bloody day, and defeat to impart.

Parliament's line would occupy,

A two-mile stretch they'd fortify,

With musket, cannon and the pike,

To advance or await the Royalist strike.

But by virtue of Parliament's line being longer,

And, in numbers, they were stronger,

The Royalist left was compromised,

Could be outflanked and then chastised.

Yet one of each flank had come to rest,

On the Sulby Hedges which no one possessed,

Each side thinking their flank was barred,

As progress through hedges would be hard.

As the day grew lighter, cannon erupted,

The still of the morning suddenly disrupted.

Men prayed to God as their soul's trustee:

'If I forget thee Lord, please don't forget me!'

The Royalist troops were the first to proceed,

Their centre advancing by foot and by steed,

To close with the Roundheads to contend,

Their stand on the crest and blows to expend.

Just a few shots of cannon were fired,

Not hitting their mark as desired,

As Royalist infantry advanced up the rise,

To attack, defeat and demoralise.

So Parliament's hidden men emerged,

As the Royalist line toward them surged,

With only one volley of shot being traded,

Before the enemy's lines were invaded.

As infantry closed, swords were brought out,

As regiments of soldiers gave a shout,

And closed the gap with a final run,

Some using the butt of their obsolete gun.

The fighting all too quickly became,

Personal, close as each sort to aim,

A deadly blow to those they could reach,

Stabbing and clubbing to make a beach.

The Royalist infantry fought with skill,

Combined with zeal and determined will,

Forcing Parliament's men to retreat,

Their troops unable to stand or compete.

Parliament's leader, Skippon was hurt,

But he managed a panic to avert,

Withdrawing in order, although hard pressed,

Leading his men with a wound in his chest.

On Parliament's left, the cavalry engaged,

With a brutal struggle with horsemen waged,

But Parliament's Ireton beat his rival,

Then led the charge to the centre's survival.

But the Royalist infantry beat this too,

And Ireton's charge failed to undo,

Defeat in the centre which had appeared,

And loss of the battle which had reared.

Then again, the Royalist cavalry attacked,

All with the thought of victory backed,

With Ireton's wing finally wrecked,

And the Royalist right advancing unchecked.

Yet success on the Royalist right obtained,

A chase which the Cavalier's sustained,

For their success on the Royalist right,

Meant Ireton's force was chased out of sight.

And Ireton's force kept riding until,

No Royalist was chasing them for the kill,

Leading the Royalist cavalry away,

From the heat of battle and the affray.

On Parliament's right, Cromwell observed,

His disciplined line firmly preserved,

As Royalists under Langdale stared,

And their own attack soon prepared.

But Cromwell's force held its own,

Until the enemy's plans were known.

So when the Royalist charge was presented,

His attack had the Royalist planning dented.

Cromwell outnumbered his foe two to one,

With the Royalist cavalry having to run,

Up a slope on ground that was rough,

Making Langdale's assault very tough.

Orderly ranks began to break,

As riders and horses tried to make,

An attack which might have a chance,

That might help the centre to advance.

Langdale's cavalry had their flank turned,

And his troopers brutally learned,

What Cromwell's disciplined men could achieve,

Leaving so many to run and grieve.

With the Royalist left quickly routed,

Cromwell's success on the wing undoubted,

He sent a small force to pursue and chase,

Those cavaliers who'd retreated apace.

Then Cromwell turned his force which remained,

Most of his cavalry who were not drained,

Towards the foe's centre and rear,

Spreading much worry alarm and fear.

From Sulby Hedges, there then appeared,

Parliament's dragoons who were cleared,

To attack the right and to descend,

On frightened Royalists who tried to defend.

Some of Ireton's cavalry regrouped,

And now upon the Royalists swooped,

Adding to the Royalist's concern,

Whose mood had changed from being stern.

With the Royalist infantry hit from each side,

The army of Parliament turned the tide.

Desperate men asked for quarter,

Fearing they'd fall to the general slaughter.

Some tried to make a fighting retreat,

As comrades fell around at their feet.

Prince Rupert's bluecoat regiment stood,

Giving an account that was noble and good.

Refusing quarter, they presented a wall,

Which, very slowly, began to fall.

Then Fairfax himself led his regiments in,

To finish their ranks which had grown very thin.

By now the king had left his station,

Been forced to leave the operation,

By a Scottish noble who said in one breath:

'Would you go upon your death?'

For Charles himself had wanted to take,

His own lifeguard and attack for the sake,

Of all the troops he could see were taking,

The last attack, which he wasn't forsaking.

But Charles was forced to run with them all,

Though the act would shock and appal.

Forced to flee from Parliament's grasp,

With only the thought of defeat to clasp.

Meanwhile Rupert reached Parliament's baggage,

But, despite attacks, could not manage,

To force any Roundhead guard or defender,

Their precious stores to give up or surrender.

Instead, Prince Rupert sought to retrace,

His path from the battle and take his place,

On the wing, which was already lost,

The line of defeat already crossed.

When Rupert arrived, he was met,

By Fairfax's force which closed the net,

Leaving the prince with one plan to adopt,

As Parliament's force could no longer be stopped.

Leaving the field like so many before,

A choice which the prince could only abhor,

Rupert took his troops beyond,

Parliament's troops lest they should respond.

Royalist troops were soon being hounded,

Stragglers hunted, run down and surrounded.

For all of those who couldn't move faster,

There was the threat of death and disaster.

Some of the Royalists tried to stand,

When fear of death had been fanned,

But Roundheads slaughtered all who stayed,

Even camp followers who also paid.

Roundhead leaders were so enraptured,

With so many Royalists killed or captured.

A veteran army completely extinguished,

While the New Model army was distinguished.

Parliament's victory was emphatic,

Leaving their side feeling ecstatic,

Believing the battle had signified,

Their cause was right and justified.

For captured letters of Charles were disclosed,

In which a heinous plot was exposed,

Which spoke of the king's consultation,

With the Irish Catholic Confederation.

Charles had played for Catholic support,

That Parliament's strength might be short,

Asking for troops so he could frustrate,

Parliament's grip and its power abate.

In the letters, it plainly showed,

How plots with Catholics had been sowed,

Showing that Charles would do anything,

At the nation's expense to remain their king.

With the cream of the Royalist army destroyed,

The Royalist cause could not avoid,

The path that led to ruination,

And their struggle's culmination.

Too much at Naseby had been demolished,

With Royalist hopes all but abolished.

All the events which were to follow,

Proved, for Charles, very hard to swallow.

Charles Surrenders to the Scots

For Parliament, victory was to be gained,

By sending its forces unrestrained,

Through the counties and then appearing,

In strongholds where Royalists were domineering.

Mopping up forces, or some siege to tighten,

To show their strength and also to frighten,

The foe into seeing their situation,

That might bring about the war's cessation.

The New Model Army marched to the west,

To relieve Taunton, which was distressed,

By Goring's Royalists who had ensured,

A siege which Parliament's men endured.

Roundheads took Yeovil on the eighth of July,

In a move the Royalists could not deny,

As their forces were weaker and lacked resolve,

As strength and will came to dissolve.

A Royalist unit of cavalry was sent,

To Taunton that it might prevent,

Parliament's move to the town,

But the Royalist force was soon tracked down.

Yet this was only a minor diversion,

Whose outcome was never really certain,

And left the main force of Royalists weakened,

As their dire position only deepened.

On the tenth of July, the Royalists found,

They, by a battle, would be bound,

With the army of Fairfax now adjacent,

And Goring knew he could not be complacent.

But despite the effort, his force simply lacked,

The discipline by which Fairfax was backed.

Goring's men mostly broke and ran,

With Cromwell's cavalry pursuing each man.

The New Model Army simply brushed aside,

The Royalist army in its stride.

This was the last main army Charles had,

Though its training and discipline were very bad.

Then to add to the terror, clubmen joined in,

Locals who'd suffered every kind of sin,

Against their homes by the troop's violation,

And clubmen murdered with wild elation.

The defeat of Goring was another blow,

To Royalist morale already low.

Through the west, Fairfax proceeded,

As town after town quickly conceded.

When sixteen forty-five had ended,

A cloud of defeat had descended,

Upon the Royalists and their crusade,

Which looked as if it would die and fade.

In September forty-five, Bristol surrendered,

When it was stormed, and terms were tendered.

A place of imports and production,

The Royalist cause felt its reduction.

Only garrisons were left to struggle and strive,

Left alone to wait for the foe to arrive,

And then to ponder and decide,

Whether to fight or resistance provide.

Royalist garrisons were left isolated,

As Parliament's forces then concentrated,

To take their defence by siege and storm,

To starve them out, or attacks to perform.

Castles and strongholds were beset,

By Parliament's forces who hoped to get,

A victory and a quick solution,

To further the Royalist dissolution.

Corfe Castle in Dorset was one such place,

Which early in the war had to face,

A siege by Roundheads, but saw relief,

When Royalist forces ended their grief.

But now it was one of a few which subsisted,

A stronghold in Dorset that stood unassisted,

So Parliament's troops once more enclosed,

The walls of the castle and a siege was imposed.

But it wasn't the cannon which made it fall,

Not massed attacks which breached the wall,

But one of the garrison who had betrayed,

Those inside to let Roundheads invade.

One by one, the garrisons fell,

Step by step, they broke the spell,

Of notions their king had of glory,

The facts now showing a different story.

Without a field army or the ability,

To raise another for stability,

The Royalist cause began to crumble,

To falter, crack and soon to stumble.

Yet Charles was adamant, and he persisted,

In fighting on while hope still existed,

To build a base and consolidate,

In the midlands to build and deliberate.

Yet by May of sixteen forty-six,

With Royalists exhausted and all out of tricks,

Charles moved further north and fled,

To Scottish troops where foes couldn't tread.

Charles believed he'd find a refuge,

With the Scots as part of a subterfuge,

To keep his person from Parliaments' hands,

And the pursuing Roundhead bands.

But Charles had not taken into account,

The treaty with England, which was paramount,

And had also forgotten conveniently,

How the Scots still spoke of him vehemently.

For the actions he'd taken against their church,

Had caused both England and Scotland to search,

For a way to bring their monarch to heel,

As each refused to give in and kneel.

Parliament's strength was then demonstrated,

In June when Oxford capitulated,

The capital city of Charles and his faction,

Falling to Parliament's great satisfaction.

169

The first civil war was all but finished,

With the power of Charles greatly diminished,

And the Scots held on to their king for a while,

Unsure what to do yet feeling hostile.

In January, sixteen forty-seven,

After debate and prayer to heaven,

The Scots concluded and agreed,

To England's call for the king to heed.

So Charles was duly handed to them,

To Parliament's forces to free or condemn.

A prisoner of those he'd tried to defeat,

For the rule of the nation to compete.

Believing the war had been concluded,

That peace, at last, was not excluded,

Everyone thought that words had replaced,

War which left England disgraced.

The Second Civil War (1648)

Through sixteen forty-seven, the factions debated,

In a country the war had created:

The New Model Army and its Independents,

With Royalists and Presbyterian attendants.

The army's leaders were named the Grandees,

Who sought compromise and their conscience to please,

In reaching a settlement with Charles as their lord,

With offers which might strike a chord.

Yet Independents of the army's troops,

Would meet in large demanding groups,

Calling for justice and reform,

Whipping up a political storm.

At Putney, in London, the army had made,

Its own headquarters and attention was paid,

To men who spoke of a constitution,

With votes, laws and less persecution.

Calling themselves Levellers, they supposed,

That things would be different, and proposed,

A new constitution, with more equality,

And votes for all men with their polity.

Presbyterians were religious and also zealous,

Protestant reformers who were seen as jealous,

Of the other groups who negotiated,

With Charles while they sat and simply waited.

With Scotland's Kirk, they did their best,

To speak with the king at his behest,

Hoping a deal could be planted,

With power to them being granted.

Then there remained the Royalists, who,

The sword for Charles willingly drew,

And now they wanted to have their say,

Not wishing their master to betray.

Though they had lost, their war never ceased,

A political struggle until Charles was released.

With all the factions they spoke and they watched,

Hoping the opponent's scheme would be botched.

For all the factions believed and cherished,

The role of king hadn't yet perished,

A necessary part of the English state,

Whether foolish, wise, humble or great.

So while they jostled to get his attention,

Charles played them all with the pretension,

That he was serious in his replies,

Knowing full well that he was their prize.

Charles was passed into each waiting hand,

So they could make their king understand,

That theirs was the path for him to take,

To accept their terms and the past forsake.

Charles could see a vacuum prevailed,

A struggle for power he worked, and he scaled.

Working each faction so he could exploit,

Their distrust of each other, at which he was adroit.

In June of forty-seven, Charles was seized,

By the army leaving many displeased,

For everyone wanted to have control,

Without one faction having the whole.

The gap between Parliament's Presbyterians,

And the army's ways so totalitarian,

Was widening more with each passing week,

Until they'd hardly listen or speak.

174

Parliament tried to have units disbanded,

As those in the Commons had already branded,

The army as radical and wanting much change,

The political structure to then rearrange.

Presbyterians in Parliament soon discussed,

With those in Scotland for a joint thrust,

To put an end to the army's prominence,

To fight a war for dominance.

And while the factions argued their point,

Their common cause was then out of joint,

So from Hampton Court, Charles slipped the ties,

In November, exposing his scheme and lies.

Slipping security, which wasn't tight,

He got away to the Isle of Wight,

To Carisbrooke Castle across the Solent,

Expecting support at any moment.

Negotiations with Scotland then were held,

With Scottish fears of Charles dispelled,

If he would help with the kirk's transforming,

So the Scots, to Charles, were slowly warming.

All too soon, the lines were drawn,

With the veil of negotiation torn.

When Scotland's Parliament he been swayed.

Scotland sent an army to Charles' aid,

By the summer of sixteen forty-eight,

Charles was right to celebrate,

His change in fortune he'd engineered,

The uncertain path that disappeared.

Across the nation, Royalists flocked,

To fight for a cause now again unlocked.

Rising up once more in bloody duel,

With Roundheads in a war so cruel.

Scottish troops, as promised, invaded,

Whilst elated Royalist units paraded,

Keen to fight for their king once more,

Upholding the oath which they swore.

Yet while the troops were enthusiastic,

In taking actions that were so drastic,

Few could hope to defeat or match,

New Model troops and tactics they'd hatch.

For many Royalists, defeat was swift,

Death and imprisonment their only gift.

Hardship and misery was in store,

For daring to make more civil war.

Yet again, the civil war would involve,

Protracted sieges which would evolve,

Into a war of patience and nerve,

Each side relying on their own reserve.

But Cromwell and Fairfax were never furtive,

And both were brisk in being assertive,

Reducing forces or strongholds they faced,

Until the threat was crushed and erased.

Scotland's army presented a threat,

Veteran troops who upon them would set,

In pitched battles to decide,

Who, with power, would preside.

The Duke of Hamilton was at the head,

Of once Scottish allies who'd engaged instead,

To fight for the king and secure liberation,

For the man who'd caused them aggravation.

By August, Lancashire towns were approached

Preston itself being encroached,

And it seemed as if the Scottish progression,

Would finally see the Roundhead's suppression.

Dubbed Engagers for having dropped,

Links with Roundheads and having swapped,

Their allegiance to what, by most, was seen,

As a fight against a monarch so mean.

Now they approached as the invaders,

A foreign army of Scottish raiders,

Intent on undoing all their endeavour,

Destroying Parliament's role forever.

So General Cromwell with the troops was sent,

This act of invasion to prevent.

He knew the consequence of any failure,

Knew he'd be Parliament's saviour.

The Battle of Preston (Aug. 1648)

Cromwell had learnt of his enemy's pace,

Felt confident his troops were ready to face,

Whatever force the Scots might display,

Needing to crush it without delay.

Scouts and informers had supplied,

Information that was applied,

To help the Roundheads ascertain,

Where the Scots were, and advantage gain.

They learnt that Hamilton's Scots were set,

To engage the Roundheads and quickly get,

A victory to clear their southern procession,

To give their king his realm's possession.

Having near eleven thousand to feed,

Hamilton's men would soon feel the need,

Of all the supplies to keep the men going,

So were badly strung out with progress slowing.

Some of the officers thought it unwise,

To string the men out for all their supplies,

As if their position was then discovered,

Their weakened state might not be recovered.

The main body of Scots was badly strung out,

Not knowing that Cromwell was about.

Thousands of troops on the Wigan road,

Not ready for battle if the enemy showed.

Cromwell had marched down the Ribble valley,

His disciplined units not needing to rally.

And as they approached Preston Moor,

Hamilton's position was no longer obscure.

Under Langdale, a Royalist, they tried to disturb,

The Roundhead advance and its movement to curb.

Just three thousand infantry who were stunned,

With five hundred cavalry, all outgunned.

With almost nine thousand at his disposal,

Cromwell put forward a simple proposal.

His men would advance, with foes extinguished,

And his men in battle would be distinguished.

For four long hours, the Royalists resisted,

Roundhead assaults which persisted.

Four long hours which Royalists bought,

Yet their sacrifice would come to naught.

Royalists were pushed to the Ribble River,

To die or themselves to the foe deliver.

Then Cromwell found he was free to cross,

The two main bridges to Hamilton's loss.

The Ribble and Darwen bridges were,

Taken by Cromwell so he could transfer,

His men across and then make haste,

In pursuing the Scots, who he rapidly chased.

Strung out along the road and unnerved,

A bad defeat to Scotland was served,

With those who stood to fight being slain,

While most surrendered to avoid the pain.

Royalist troops dropped musket and pike,

No longer aggressive or feeling warlike,

Hoping roundheads would then reveal,

Mercy to end their sad ordeal.

Most of the Royalists took this path,

Avoiding the enemy's murderous wrath.

Yet, for some the choice they made to quit,

Was not enough to death outwit.

Two thousand were killed trying to halt,

The Roundhead advance and their assault,

While nine thousand more chose to surrender,

Aware their chances of mercy were slender.

When the first civil war had come to an end,

These Royalists promised to suspend,

All future acts that were aggressive,

Then broke their word in acts so excessive.

They'd lost the war and were paroled,

Giving promises they'd never hold,

So brutal justice was their lot,

With many leaders being shot.

Some cavaliers were simply banished,

To the new world where they vanished.

Lost to a colony n'er to return,

Longing for loved ones for whom they'd yearn.

With two thousand killed, and nine thousand bagged,

Scottish and Royalist hopes soon sagged.

Cromwell's victory was momentous,

But for the king was portentous.

With the army of Scotland brutally crushed,

The Royalist voice was all but hushed.

A few small forces carried on striving,

But none were too long in the surviving.

Charles had gambled away his last chance,

Drastically changed his circumstance.

The second civil war would come to an end,

In a way that Charles could not comprehend.

In December, with Charles again apprehended,

The army's attitude to him was amended.

They finally saw what lengths he'd go to,

And their dealings with him they'd have to review.

For now, as their prisoner, he was installed,

At Windsor Castle, which was well walled,

So that the army could keep their prize safe,

A prisoner which made them swear and chafe.

Rump Parliament

With the ways of their king so unmasked,

Many of Parliament's people asked,

Whether Charles should be reinstated,

When his lack of respect was well illustrated.

The army too were clearly aware,

That their monarch had a flair,

For showing all just to what extent,

He'd stoop for his power to augment.

He'd taken up arms to hopefully thwart,

The rights of Parliament, with hopes to extort,

Their acknowledgement and submission,

That he was master with their recognition.

Many thousands of lives had been ended,

With normal life being suspended,

As each side fought to at last emerge,

As victorious, taking all to the verge.

Yet still there were those who tried to insist,

They had to negotiate, turn and twist,

In order to reach a lasting accord,

That every path must be explored.

Men like Fairfax then asserted,

Negotiation should not be deserted,

And a deal with the king was their only choice,

If the army, and Parliament, were to have a voice.

For them, the role of king was essential,

Showing that they were still deferential.

An England without monarchs was outrageous,

New, untried and not advantageous.

So Parliament tried once more to talk,

Once more on the path of compromise walk,

To see if they could reach an arrangement,

To end this bad and mutual estrangement.

But the army, finally, had had its fill,

Of the Commons trying to negotiate still,

So troops then marched upon that space,

Which many believed was the army's base.

Thomas Pride commanded this purge,

Outraged that the house would urge,

More talk and more negotiation,

Knowing the end to be stagnation.

Only seventy-five members were allowed,

To remain in Parliament and were endowed,

With the army's powerful backing,

Its determination never slacking.

For most of the Commons were accused,

Of wanting to talk, and were refused,

Their seat in the house so they could bend,

To whatever terms their king might send.

In December, Parliament was cut to a rump,

Which, to the army's voice, must jump,

For power rested in the army's embrace,

Who refused their sacrifice to debase.

Then, at the army's forceful bidding,

Once the Commons had had the clipping,

The Rump of Parliament was directed,

That Charles to justice should be subjected.

The move on Parliament had been precise,

But also came with a big price,

When Fairfax, who had argued most,

Told the Rump parliament he'd leave his post.

He disagreed with the army's decision,

And soon was set for a collision,

With those whose ideas he saw as severe,

To which he'd never choose to adhere.

So, this leader of the army resigned,

In a move the army never designed,

Leaving a space which had to be filled,

By Cromwell, who was equally skilled.

Trial of a King (Jan. 1649)

Then the Rump Parliament received its directive,

Issued by the army from their perspective,

Which saw the king as the perpetrator,

Of all the suffering and was a traitor.

The army believed it had good reason,

To charge the king on the grounds of treason,

Believing Charles had caused the ordeal,

And intrigues and plots to conceal.

The soldiers saw Charles as cunning and vile,

So wanted to see their king stand on trial.

In the name of the people, a high court met,

With the case against Charles hastily set.

A Bill through Parliament hoped to spark,

The common interest so they could embark,

Upon the trial, but many opposed,

To ideas that Charles should be deposed.

Yet the Bill went through, and he was arraigned,

With the army's plan no longer constrained.

Without the Lords or royal approval,

The army was planning for the king's removal.

The twentieth of January, sixteen forty-nine,

In Westminster Hall, where monarchs would dine,

Sixty-eight commissioners had convened,

To try the man they saw as a fiend.

Solicitor General, John Cook, tried to speak,

But Charles, who was close, and full of critique,

Tried to say something, but was ignored,

So hit Cook with his cane as his reward.

The head of the cane snapped on Cook's shoulder,

Sat there, untouched, then retrieved by Cook's scolder,

Who stood, amazed, that nobody jumped,

Or at his feet as supplicants slumped.

When Cook finished speaking, Charles was expected,

To enter a plea, but instead objected,

To all the proceedings he said were unjust,

The divine right of kings they should trust.

He declared that he, by God, was anointed,

To rule as king and so appointed,

To have authority by law and tradition,

Not needing anyone else's permission.

Charles told them they had no jurisdiction,

To try their king or gain a conviction,

Saying the court was really illegal,

As God decided who was to be regal.

Charles maintained they were incorrect,

If they felt they could the law neglect,

Asking by what authority they sat,

To make the decision they would arrive at.

So Charles refused to recognise,

Or even his plea to revise,

Not pleading guilt or innocence,

Just seeing the judge's insolence.

The court was quick in then disputing,

All Charles said and also refuting,

Trying to prove and then convince,

That he was on trial though he was their prince.

The case against Charles was swiftly built,

Though Charles didn't show any sign of guilt.

Thirty witnesses would testify,

To crimes of the king, but many would lie.

Witnesses spoke in a different room,

Where MP's and lawyers could lead and groom,

So Charles didn't have a chance to reject,

A prosecution which was partly suspect.

But the army had planned to sacrifice,

Their king in a trial which was concise.

Charles was found guilty seven days later,

As England's tyrant and violator.

Only fifty-nine men were ready and willing,

To sign as commissioners for the blood spilling.

Men who were ready to give their name,

To confirm that Charles was solely to blame.

Many men were troubled were worried,

Lest a verdict on Charles by them was hurried,

But Cromwell would to the judges admit,

They'd cut off his head with the crown upon it.

In a verdict which many Royalists dreaded,

Charles was guilty, and would be beheaded,

On the thirtieth of January where crowds would flock,

Most there to weep, and a few just to mock.

The Palace of Whitehall was the place selected,

The Banqueting House with a scaffold erected.

There in front of a waiting crowd,

Charles, at last, to speak was allowed.

Addressing the crowd, which numbered many,

He said he sought liberty as much as any.

He spoke of the difference between subjects and kings,

'A subject and a sovereign are clean different things.'

He wore a thick shirt as the morning was cold,

So not to shiver then wore the blindfold,

Stretched out his arms, and awaited the axe,

Which, in one strike, made the body relax.

In death, the king was seen as brave,

And the execution caused a shock wave,

Amongst the Royalists who still intended,

That the state of England should be amended.

Aftermath (Jan. 1649 – Sept. 1651)

The people of Britain had been subjected,

To brutal war and also infected,

By deadly disease which laid many low,

Filling the nation with death and woe.

Not only the soldiers were those to suffer,

Civilians too finding things tougher,

As men from all armies often wondered,

If the towns they were near could be plundered.

Men wounded in battle would fall and stare,

At the gaping flesh laid bleeding and bare,

Numbed, then feeling the pain increase,

Agony begging for death's release.

Countless women in sorrow were draped,

Losing their men or brutally raped,

By soldiers who saw each woman they met,

As something for use without regret.

All the people of Britain despaired,

At the loss and all the pain they shared.

At last the war had found a conclusion,

Ending death's might and profusion.

But Charles the First had a loyal son,

Also named Charles through whom would run,

A desire for revenge which daily burned,

And who, for the crown, was also concerned.

Just a few weeks after his father was slain,

Still reeling from the grief and pain,

Prince Charles was named Charles the Second,

With all the hope this action beckoned.

The only choice the new king had now,

Was to turn to Scotland and make a vow,

To do as they asked and demanded,

Or walk away empty handed.

Sent by the father to live in exile,

King Charles, to the Commons, was also hostile,

With the death of his father adding weight,

To the Royalist cause which they tried to negate.

Charles was the crown's lawful heir,

So he would have to risk and dare,

A scheme to help him work toward,

A plan to see his rights restored.

Scotland was the only option,

If they agreed to the plan's adoption,

As they had an army which could be employed,

To help King Charles more exile avoid.

The death of his father had ignited,

Scotland's outrage and then united,

Kirk and Parliament as never before,

To address this act they couldn't ignore.

Scotland itself had been afflicted,

Through civil war with death inflicted,

By Covenanters and those who were loyal,

To Charles the First and all that was royal.

In June, sixteen fifty, Charles the Second landed,

In the north of Scotland and immediately handed,

Ideas of concessions which he would grant,

To the National and Solemn League Covenant.

Through this Charles promised to allow,

Presbyterian reform and made a vow,

To let reform in England spread,

More church reform to go ahead.

Negotiations were long and also hard,

With Charles, it seemed, forced to discard,

Much authority to Scottish pressing,

Yet his dream of victory was progressing.

With an army behind him, Charles became,

A threat which England had to tame,

For England's Republic was still only young,

And the people's faith in it could be swung.

Meanwhile, in Ireland, trouble was brewing,

With continued war the nation's undoing,

As the fighting there was left to wage,

From sixteen forty-one in a long rampage.

But the arrest of Charles the First set in motion,

A wave of thought to end the devotion,

Of fighting each other with little result,

But instead with each other to talk and consult.

For despite it all, he was still their sovereign,

And any new rule was seen as foreign,

So the fighting factions became united,

That release of their king be expedited.

Royalists and Confederates joined as one,

To defeat the Roundheads 'til they were undone.

At Dublin, the Irish tried to blockade,

Parliament's forces who weren't dismayed.

Yet by August forty-nine, the siege was broken,

Word of the New Model Army spoken.

Cromwell landed at Dublin to join the pursuit,

To hunt down the rebels and end the dispute.

By September forty-nine, in a town by the coast,

The Irish, at Drogheda, would suffer the most,

When Cromwell's troops stormed and forced,

The walls killing thousands, which Cromwell endorsed.

Afterwards, he stated that they were all armed,

Why so many people were killed or harmed.

But the Irish people would always remember,

English aggression in that bloody September.

Cromwell's campaign in Ireland was ruthless,

All Irish resistance proving too useless,

As his skill and his disciplined troops demonstrated,

Leaving all Irish hopes devastated.

By May sixteen fifty, Cromwell turned to,

The Scottish threat which steadily grew.

Crossing the Irish Sea to confront,

Charles and the Scots which he'd have to hunt.

By now the Scots had loudly proclaimed,

That Charles, their prince, should be named,

As king of Great Britain, Ireland and France,

Clearly showing to England their Royalist stance.

July saw Cromwell at Edinburgh's gates,

But lack of supplies left his army in straits,

So, by late August, the siege was lifted,

To retreat to Dunbar where supplies had shifted.

By early September, a Scots army appeared,

When Cromwell's army to Dunbar neared,

But Cromwell's veterans were soon deployed,

And the Scottish army was soundly destroyed.

With Cromwell's army and supplies intact,

He returned to Edinburgh, and defenders cracked.

By the end of that year, southern Scotland saw,

The New Model Army, leaving many in awe.

Leaving one of his generals to mop up the foe,

In sixteen fifty-one, Cromwell would go,

On a march to find and then to defeat,

King Charles the Second, and success to complete.

In July he crossed the Firth of Forth,

Taking his army further north,

And at Inverkeithing, the Roundheads ensured,

That another defeat for the Scots was endured.

But as the New Model advanced to Perth,

Charles moved south to show his worth,

To any Royalists who cared to rebel,

Who chose the Royalist ranks to swell.

Marching to England's north and west,

He put old loyalties to the test,

By his and his army's sudden appearance,

Asking for his cause's adherence.

Yet all the support Charles expected,

Wasn't forthcoming and barely detected,

As many people were sick of the wars,

Preoccupied with life and its daily chores.

But Cromwell was already on his trail,

Determined, again, not to fail,

In bringing his foe to bloody battle,

In hearing his enemy's last death rattle.

By September, Cromwell had closed,

The threat of his army clearly posed,

And, at Worcester, Charles comprehended,

His path further south could not be extended.

Each day the Roundheads marched twenty miles,

Through summer sun in military files,

To catch the enemy in their grip,

Hoping their foe wouldn't give them the slip.

This force with which the Roundheads would clash,

This Scottish invasion they sought to smash,

Was already weakened and feeling the strain,

From a long and fruitless summer campaign.

For the lack of interest shown to the Scots,

From English who wouldn't risk the shots,

Sapped the morale which gradually faded,

As fewer men by their cause were persuaded.

Local Englishmen had taken offence,

That the foreign army had the pretence,

Of being a force of liberation,

With Charles expecting more adoration.

Soon the Scots found themselves alone,

With little help or assistance shown,

Knowing that Cromwell's wrath was descending,

And bloody battle was impending.

Charles hoped London might be an objective,

But he knew the plan would be defective,

As his army was tired and needed to spend,

Time to rest and itself to mend.

So he'd gone to Worcester to recuperate,

Hoping to rest and accommodate,

All his men and then to provoke,

The flames of the Royalist cause to stoke.

Cromwell sent troops through the countryside,

Knowing the Scots couldn't hide,

From the judgement he hope to acquire,

Justice born from the blade and gunfire.

On the third of September, tension heightened,

When Cromwell's force around Worcester tightened,

With part deployed to stop Charles advocating,

Withdrawing and Worcester's evacuating.

With all his forces then situated,

His plans for attack calculated,

Cromwell himself would then conduct,

The attack which Charles would try to obstruct.

The River Severn and the River Teme,

Had to be crossed in Cromwell's scheme,

So units were trained to help him span,

The rivers which through his offensive ran.

Roundheads were now on the left and right bank,

Advancing to Worcester as resistance shrank.

But their advance was fiercely contested,

By Royalists who hoped it would be arrested.

Some Royalist units in Worcester had striven,

To break out of town, but then were driven,

Back to their lines by Roundheads who'd headed,

To block the escape which Royalists dreaded.

Outnumbered, the Royalists also incurred,

A brutal assault but went on undeterred.

But the skill and discipline of the aggressor,

Meant their foe would be Victory's possessor.

As darkness fell, many Royalists slipped,

Through enemy lines as panic gripped.

Yet locals too joined the chase for the hunted,

Not afraid that stragglers should be confronted.

Darkness and disaster enveloped,

Royalist troops as defeat developed.

Despite their brave and determined stance,

Against Cromwell's troops there wasn't much chance.

Despite it all, Charles succeeded,

In escaping the net almost unheeded,

Legend saying he hid in a tree,

In large oak branches as a refugee.

Roundhead cavalry scoured and searched,

But never saw Charles in the tree he was perched.

He slipped through patrols, and got away safely,

To foreign shores and relative safety.

Charles and the Scots had tried to slay,

Parliament's strength and in the grave lay,

The rights of The Commons and reinvent,

Their own Royal power, and strength to cement.

But the plan of Charles was ill conceived,

As Royalist hopes were not retrieved,

And Charles was forced to run and affirm,

Parliament's power in the long term.

Whatever decision Charles would choose,

Against the foe he was bound to lose,

As the New Model Army under Cromwell displayed,

That he and his troops knew their trade.

Long before Charles had fought and escaped,

England, in Parliament's power, was draped.

A new Republic had already ascended,

With Royalist power now seemingly ended.

Oliver Cromwell-General & Protector

In April of fifteen ninety-nine,

When Tudor power was in decline,

He entered a world that wholly embraced,

Religious beliefs which life interlaced.

Born at the end of the Tudor reign,

To a Huntingdon family that was rather plain,

Modest gentry who could clearly trace,

Their line to Cromwell who served the Kings grace.

Daily life by belief was consumed,

The mercy and love of God presumed,

With everyone hoping to finally dwell,

With God in heaven, and not Satan in hell.

So Oliver was to this faith exposed,

To acts of heresy stoutly opposed,

Being imbued with a strong devotion,

To the protestant cause and its promotion.

As a young man, he'd worship and praise,

God above in definite ways,

Showing a faith that was simple and pure,

A belief in God that would endure.

Then, in his thirties, he underwent,

A deeply personal, spiritual event,

When he had a religious conversion,

Leading him to a puritan immersion.

An independent puritan full of fire,

Who worked for God and hoped to aspire,

To a higher plane once faith was planted,

That a glimpse of God might then be granted.

215

By sixteen twenty, he'd gained a wife,

Elizabeth Bourchier, to share his life,

And over the years, nine children were born,

Three dying young and from them torn.

Elizabeth's father had good connections,

To Puritan gentry and their directions,

Towards a better system of rule,

Which would young Oliver's passion fuel.

In sixteen twenty-eight he was elected,

As MP for Huntingdon and was projected,

Onto the Stuart political scene,

Which to improve he was very keen.

Yet Oliver had a time of despair,

Doubts and depression, he couldn't bear,

A personal crisis which he weathered,

His faith in religion temporarily severed.

Some said that part of his problem's root,

Was based on the gentry and a dispute,

He had with them over a new town charter,

Their disagreement becoming sharper.

Summoned before the Privy Council,

Oliver's problem became financial.

He had to sell properties he'd acquired,

A step down in society he hadn't desired.

But though his status seemed reduced,

Enough wealth for a gentleman was produced,

And though he resembled a yeoman farmer,

Oliver felt clad in God's strong armour.

In time, with help, a new faith sprung,

Deep, powerful and always young,

With which he'd use to justify,

His path in life and battle cry.

Deeply religious, it was felt by some,

As if a new Moses on earth had come,

When he rose to become a prominent soldier,

A burden that he alone could shoulder.

Believing he'd been a terrible sinner,

Now he felt he was the winner,

Of revelation which his soul would adorn,

As 'the congregation of the firstborn'.

Confident, Oliver thought to leave,

For the Americas and there to retrieve,

His status and his livelihood,

For his, and his family's, ultimate good.

But fate was about to intervene,

Which Oliver didn't contravene,

When he, by Parliament, was prevented,

From leaving England which he lamented.

Then fate delivered one more thing,

Which would to Oliver fortune bring,

With an uncle's property in Ely inherited,

Which Oliver thought by God was merited.

By sixteen forty, King Charles had ruled,

For years by himself, but the fire hadn't cooled,

As militant puritans hadn't forgotten,

All their king's faults they saw as rotten.

As MP for Cambridge, Oliver headed,

From Ely to London where was embedded,

All the intrigue of political suspense,

Where the great divide would soon commence.

Sitting alongside his puritan brothers,

Some saying he owed his position to others,

Oliver tried to ignore the rumour,

That he owed his seat to some gentleman's humour.

But when war with the king was finally entered,

Oliver, for the Parliament, ventured,

To show his belief for reform was sincere,

And that his commitment would never veer.

Throughout the war, he steadily rose,

Despite all hardship, highs and lows,

Showing his skill in all warfare,

In which few of the time could compare.

From Marston Moor to Naseby's bloodletting,

Oliver showed that he was getting,

Results on the battlefield which were superior,

To Royalist ways which were inferior.

With no formal training in war and tactics,

His men were seen as Roundhead fanatics,

Deeply committed to the man they admired,

Whose natural leadership moved and inspired.

With the New Model Army for him to lead,

The soldiers of England became a new breed,

Of troops who were feared and respected,

Their skill at arms slowly perfected.

Discipline, faith and innovation,

Were Oliver's traits, and an indication,

That he believed he worked to God's dream,

And that he must his nation redeem.

All of his foes would learn to greet,

The anguish of their swift defeat,

As Oliver's troops gave their instruction,

On how to deliver swift destruction.

Sixteen forty-seven, saw much confusion,

With Parliament causing great disillusion,

When various leaders talked and contended,

That their stance with Charles must be amended.

Some sought a risky reconciliation,

With the army's rapid demobilisation,

With the New Model Army being disbanded,

With the king hardly being reprimanded.

Levellers wanted greater change,

Seeing the dealings with Charles as strange,

As they had fought for their own liberation,

Not for liberty's condemnation.

Oliver wanted to make a good deal,

Which, to all factions, might appeal,

So he had proposals finely drafted,

Words of wisdom cleverly crafted.

By now the army had Charles in their clutch,

That other factions were unable to touch,

Or get too near and to him assure,

They could the right of king procure.

Yet Charles gave all his captors the slip,

Escaping from the army's grip.

By sixteen forty-eight, war was entered,

Upon the right to rule still centred.

Oliver set off with the army again,

Hoping this new threat to contain,

Willing and able to show all who chose,

What awaited for them who dared to oppose.

All through that year, Oliver raced,

To key locations where resistance was placed,

Defeating the Royalists one by one,

Until the bloody path was run.

Then, at Preston, with the army he led,

The Royalist force was cut to a shred,

By the tactics and skill Oliver used,

Which left the enemy bloodied and bruised.

He believed his success was clearly sent,

From heaven above and God's intent,

In using key men to bring about,

A land which was worthy and devout.

Letters he wrote encouraged the reader,

To have faith in God as their true leader.

Oliver used faith as his mighty shield,

The Word of God the weapon he'd wield.

When Charles was tried and sentenced to die,

Some of his foes would talk and try,

To find a way out of signing the warrant,

That would see his blood flow in a torrent.

Yet Oliver was the third who signed,

Which their king to death assigned.

Reluctant men were forced to decide,

Signing the warrant for regicide.

Once Charles was beheaded, a new state was declared,

A republic in which the people shared,

Or so they believed once the fighting stopped,

Once the power of kings was finally cropped.

A 'Commonwealth of England' with Parliament's rump,

The body of power cut to a stump,

That would, they thought, be a blessing,

With all the grievances soon addressing.

Oliver, with others, had been appointed,

To a council of state as England's anointed,

Guiding the nation for the common good,

With hopes for a common brotherhood.

Oliver's days of war weren't to end,

When the new regime decided to send,

Him and the army across the sea,

To Ireland to force parliamentary decree.

He showed the Catholics little mercy,

His actions gaining much controversy.

Civilians were slaughtered along with the rest,

Yet Oliver believed his actions were blessed.

When the Irish rebel force was broken,

And tales of English zeal were spoken,

The army, once more, had to embark,

To friendly shores to stamp their mark.

Scottish troops had penetrated,

Onto English soil and intimidated.

All true Englishmen were incensed,

So the wrath of Oliver was dispensed.

Defeat on the Scots looked to be crushing,

Survivors eager to be homewards rushing.

Cromwell's name they wouldn't forget,

In Scottish and Irish history set.

In the two years that Oliver was absent,

MP's had fallen into much dissent.

With the head of the Royalist cause terminated,

Division and gain were motivated.

He tried to get parliament to implement,

Reforms and not be ambivalent,

To what he believed the people required,

And to show the nation faith hadn't expired.

Annoyed by the Rump's blinkered stance,

Oliver gave it one last chance,

To show this Barebones was really caring,

That policy could be great and daring.

The Lord Protector (1653 – 1658)

In sixteen fifty-three, he demanded,

The Rump disband and then be handed,

To a caretaker power that was a construction,

Of MP's and army who might suffer instruction.

Consisting of just forty seats,

Oliver hoped there'd be no repeats,

Of debates and Bills which only ignored,

The England he hoped to move toward.

But the Rump returned to its own debating,

Its own prestige and power inflating,

So Oliver changed the situation,

Much to parliament's protestation.

With forty troops he entered the hall,

Intent on seeing that parliament fall.

Taking parliament's ceremonial mace,

He sent MP's away in disgrace.

A new assembly was to be compiled,

Who, as saints, were to be styled,

Men whose faith was pure and intense,

Who didn't show any false pretence.

But this zealous Parliament of the Saints,

Was feared too righteous and had its taints,

As radical men had the majority,

And might abuse their new authority.

This Barebones Parliament eventually voted,

That its own dissolution should be promoted.

For just a few months, MP's attended,

The parliament until it was suspended.

Then shortly after its dissolution,

They found a speedy substitution,

When John Lambert, a general, had suggested,

That power, in one, should be invested.

Oliver Cromwell was the man he named,

Pious, brave and for battle famed,

And in December it was decreed,

That as Lord Protector he should proceed.

Wearing black as a humble testimony,

He was sworn in in the ceremony,

Which made him for life the nation's protector,

It's guardian and political director.

Yet his faith was never sacrificed,

As daily he sought the wisdom of Christ,

To help him rule as he felt he should,

To lead in the way he felt God would.

Under him, a parliament was shaped,

Men whose piety around them draped,

To debate on how to build and repair,

And how to end the people's despair.

Parliament could, under him, be dissolved,

A new one formed when he felt resolved.

But he had to go through a council of state,

To get a majority to decide England's fate.

But Oliver, also, was just a person,

And temptation for power would only worsen,

With men giving honour to England's trustee,

Given wealth and signing as Oliver 'P'.

In time, he'd be offered the crown to wear,

King Oliver the First for all to declare.

Though offered, Oliver flatly refused,

Having seen the role of king so abused.

231

He saw there was a vital quest,

That must be debated and expressed,

If the nation were to ever heal,

If the republic were to all appeal.

Two priorities fixed his mind,

Which, if they were both combined,

Would make the nation heal much faster,

Settle their minds after much disaster.

Healing and settling after so much chaos,

A land so tinged with all that pathos,

Was what the Lord Protector would try,

While on his faith in God rely.

Oliver also went on to claim,

That to the nation's constant shame,

The people's moral and spiritual living,

Needed reform and God's forgiving.

He believed that if these goals were achieved,

Then God would forgive and not be aggrieved.

Oliver felt that with God's consent,

They might the wrath of God prevent.

In sixteen fifty-five, Royalists rebelled,

Hoping their rebellion spelled,

The end of the republic and the recall,

Of the monarchy that seemed to enthral.

But the planned rebellion wasn't supported,

Recruits for the Royalists couldn't be courted,

So the few who rose up were soon overcome,

Aware they'd have to flee or succumb.

Oliver decided to stop this offense,

And thought it would make very good sense,

To divide the nation into fifteen zones,

Controlled by generals, whose loyalty was known.

Major generals would rule every sector,

As guardian, watchdog and tax inspector.

But this new plan only lasted a year,

With reformists worried and experiencing fear.

The general's actions became a gift,

To Royalist hatred and opened a rift,

Between the factions which needed a cure,

In a young republic which hoped to mature.

Yet the Lord Protector still maintained,

Puritan souls should be restrained,

And not to react or be frightened,

But to walk with God and be enlightened.

To this end, he planned to invite,

The Jews back to England that they might,

Bring wealth and no longer be the pariah,

And might herald the coming of the messiah.

The Lord Protector understood,

There was always a likelihood,

That non-believers might be converted,

Their fear of the regime then deserted.

So he tried to show and demonstrate,

He could forgive and tolerate,

Any belief which had the potential,

To worship God and be reverential.

Despite his beliefs and conviction,

It never worked as a restriction,

To England's foreign policies,

Or dealing with her colonies.

A deal was struck with nearby France,

Promising English troops to enhance,

France's ongoing strife with Spain,

For Spanish loss and English gain.

In sixteen fifty-seven, during his ruling,

After months of effort that were gruelling,

The offer of king had arisen,

But Oliver wouldn't to reason listen.

He chose to remain as Protector instead,

To leave the rank of king as dead,

Believing in God's intent and salvation,

That God had determined to end that vocation.

But the ceremony did reflect,

A coronation with much respect,

With regalia which, by some, was viewed,

As royal, presumptuous and almost crude.

At Westminster Hall, on King Edward's chair,

Oliver Cromwell would promise and swear,

To follow the Humble Petition and Advice,

A constitution he could not sacrifice.

Yet with rank there came the ability,

To raise allies to the nobility,

Showering those who were true with reward,

Titles and honours he was free to award.

Under his direction, the nation earned,

Greater respect and a corner was turned,

As foreign powers were forced to concur,

That respect on England they must confer.

But like all men, the Protector was mortal,

Who longed to pass through the heavenly portal.

A man who had lived and was then getting old,

Who longed to see God and his face to behold.

In sixteen fifty-eight, the Protector grew weak,

In pain, he found it harder to speak,

And in September, after an illness,

His mind and body at last knew stillness.

Oliver Cromwell at last found peace,

Ending the burden and finding release.

He believed he knew where he belonged,

Wishing it wouldn't be prolonged.

Some would regret Oliver dying,

The man they believed was edifying,

Whilst many were happy and were elated,

Having heard of the death of him they hated.

Whatever the feeling, they had to accept,

That as a leader he wasn't inept.

In time, some critics would try to poor blame,

On the work he did and extinguish his flame.

Oliver Cromwell never sought the road,

To power or glory but had it bestowed,

By fate through unfortunate circumstance,

Perhaps by God or by fickle chance.

Yet when he was given the ultimate task,

Of ruling the nation he wouldn't bask,

In the trappings of king or what it afforded,

Believing in heaven he would be rewarded.

Not everyone cherished the puritan manner,

Resisting reform and its banner,

Preferring a life which to them was better,

To one day be free of the puritan fetter.

As many believed the life was austere,

Lacking in colour and lacking in cheer.

Their lives were there for the living,

In a world which was cruel and unforgiving.

Angry when festivals they had planned,

Like Christmas which their Parliament banned,

Unhappy people silently moaned,

That their rejoicing was postponed.

For decades the protestant leaders had,

Considered Christmas immoral and bad,

As it led the people to great excess,

To drunkenness and too much distress.

The Protector had also calculated,

That Christmas should be celebrated,

By prayer and quiet contemplation,

A Christmas with an adaptation.

With the Protector gone, hope grew keener,

Changing the people's thoughts and demeanour.

For those who stepped in filling Oliver's shoes,

Could not this wave of hope defuse.

The Restoration (May 1660)

The death of Cromwell had been quick,

An infection turning septicemic,

And the death of his daughter caused distress,

To lower his spirits and depress.

The mantle of power soon was passed,

To Richard, his son, but couldn't last,

As Richard's power base was slim,

With the prospect of success looking dim.

But he tried to go on as his father had wished,

Yet the strength of his father was sorely missed,

Leaving the new protector adrift,

Not having his father's leadership gift.

For eight long months Richard struggled,

As he led the nation and power juggled,

Doing his best to emulate,

His father's skill to arbitrate.

It seemed like the role of protector was spent,

As various factions seemed free to vent,

Thoughts of the future and their concern,

That perhaps to the past they might return.

By May of sixteen fifty-nine,

Richard's hold was in decline,

With calls for a king rapidly growing,

The wind of change steadily blowing.

The role which Richard Cromwell held,

Meant the Protector was compelled,

To face the truth, and was inclined,

To walk away and so resigned.

In exile, the King made a proclamation,

Much to the people's acclamation,

In which he promised a national pardon,

If to the Republic they all would harden.

Most in the land would soon be driven,

By knowledge that they would be forgiven,

By Charles if everyone saw and accepted,

Republic beliefs must be rejected.

General Monck, a roundhead official,

Saw this deal could be beneficial,

So had a parliament quickly arranged,

That the form of government could be exchanged.

Monck had the army at his back,

A power base no-one could crack.

His march to London was unopposed,

With plans for change soon exposed.

A parliament was formed that, it said,

Didn't owe allegiance but, instead,

Was a parliament that talked at liberty,

To clear Charles' path to victory.

Filled with Royalist sympathisers,

And the republic's critisisers,

It met to vote for the restoration,

Of Kings and republic's ruination.

The Interregnum's bold endeavour,

Had, it seemed, caused much displeasure,

As many people eagerly waited,

To see a king soon reinstated.

From the moment Charles was beheaded,

Republican thoughts were embedded,

Into the hearts and minds of those,

Who dealt with tradition's grim death throes.

But England's Republic was very young,

Its merits and virtues still unsung,

When men in power made the decision,

That England's choice needed revision.

In an age when people felt suspicion,

With anything breaking the old tradition,

Republican values only appeared,

To destroy the values they revered.

On the eighth of May, sixteen sixty,

Members of Parliament would agree,

To vote on Charles the Second's reign,

Which would the gap of years explain.

They agreed to choose an important date,

Which would in people's minds create,

Thoughts that the strange republican age,

Hadn't existed on the political stage.

So, Charles was then officially declared,

To have ruled when regicide was dared,

His reign beginning with his father's demise,

The years in between lost in disguise.

Charles the Second returned to the land,

To a welcome which was seen as grand,

As many believed that divine order,

Would be restored within England's border.

A Royalist parliament was compiled,

By the king who once was poor and exiled.

For seventeen years this parliament remained,

By the grace of God and their king ordained.

Soon the king would turn his fury,

To the men who made the court and jury,

Which sent his father to the grave,

And to many his retribution gave.

Even the dead were not to be spared,

As each, in turn, were traitors declared.

Cromwell's body was then exhumed,

As the rage of revenge in England loomed.

Though dead, his body was taken and tied,

To the scaffold while Charles watched with pride,

While corpses of men were desecrated,

That power of Kings be demonstrated.

The Stuart line was again on the throne,

The thought of Republic having flown.

Yet England's path had altered its course,

Changed by the power of parliament's force.

The Civil War Quiz

Now that the story has been told,

We saw the path to war unfold,

As king and parliament did their best,

To put the other to the test.

Back and forth their fortunes went,

With destruction to the other meant,

Doing their best to see their foe,

Reduced that they, in turn, might grow.

Over the years, politicians spoke,

Of how they felt beneath the yoke,

Of the other's oppressive grip,

Feeling the sting of oppression's whip.

Yet, throughout, each side felt,

Justice by them would be dealt,

As theirs was a cause worthy of praise,

Full of truth and righteous phrase.

Thousands joined to fight for a dream,

That their cause might rule supreme,

Laying the other side in the dust,

All of them doing what each of them must.

Of their truth, all were persuaded,

And few would let this truth be traded,

Fighting to the bitter conclusion,

Then dealing with their disillusion.

Since those sad hostilities,

Those bloody animosities,

Parliament and monarch appreciate,

That they must always collaborate.

But what if you had heard the news,

Of civil war and had to choose,

Between your monarch and parliament,

And had to join one argument?

Which, I wonder, would you select?

Which of the two would you protect?

Take the quiz and please persevere,

To see if you're Roundhead or Cavalier.

The answers you find aren't right or wrong,

As freedom of choice to each belong.

So, before you answer, please stop and peruse,

Your sense of justice in this quiz to amuse.

Quiz

1. Do you believe in the divine right of Kings?

2. How important is it to you that MPs represent the people?

3. Do you believe that everyone should be able to vote?

4. Should the king alone be allowed to raise taxes?

5. Is it important for the king to consult a parliament on anything?

6. Does the king have the right to dismiss his parliament whenever he wants to?

7. Does parliament have the right to present the king with any critical view of his rule?

8. Who should have control over the army?

9. Should parliament or the king decide policies?

10. Should only nobles be given important positions in government or the army?

11. Who should decide who the king marries?

12. Is religion an important factor when it comes to the choice of queen?

13. Should parliament be prepared to use force of arms against the king?

14. Is it right for the king to use any means at his disposal to reassert his authority?

15. Did the Roundheads have the right to put the king on trial?

16. Was it a fair trial?

17. Did the Roundheads have the right to execute their monarch?

18. Was the Republic a good or bad thing?

19. Should Oliver Cromwell have accepted the offer of King?

20. Was the Restoration of the monarchy necessary?

If you enjoyed this book, then you might also like the others in this series. They are:

Britain Through the Ages

The Tudors

A History of the USA

WW1

WW2

Overlord

Printed in Great Britain
by Amazon